Crossing

Your

Jordans

McDougal & Associates
*Servants of Christ and Stewards of the
Mysteries of God*

Crossing Your Jordans

The Now. The New. The Next.

by

Regina Blount

CROSSING YOUR JORDANS
Copyright © 2012, 2016 — by Regina Blount
ALL RIGHTS RESERVED

Cover Design by Eric Pipes, Envision Graphics
eric@envisiongraphics.net

Published by:

McDougal & Associates
18896 Greenwell Springs Road
Greenwell Springs, LA 70739
www.thepublishedword.com

McDougal & Associates is dedicated to the spreading of the Gospel of Jesus Christ to as many people as possible in the shortest time possible.

ISBN 978-1-934769-87-8
Trade Paper Edition

Printed on demand in the US, the UK and Australia
For Worldwide Distribution

Dedication

I dedicate this book to my two children, Jennifer and Brinsley:

To Jennifer, whose life has taught me so much about the faithfulness of God. It's her life, her perseverance, humor, faith and ability to see the truth that causes me to understand that her walk with God is far deeper and meaningful than I could have imagined as she grew into womanhood. There could never be anyone like her in my life. I am still learning from her and am humbled she calls me Mama.

To Brinsley, who may never be able to read a page of this book. He has taught me more about the nature and character of God in my life than any other individual. His joy in life, dedication to his convictions and ability to love others for who they are has forever changed my life. He is the personification of what we expect "Christianity" truly to be. From him, too, I keep learning, and am, once again, humbled that God chose me to give him to.

Acknowledgments

Although this book was in draft form, it laid on the shelf for six years. Acknowledging the people that finally made it a reality will, inevitably, be a small thing compared to the efforts they expended.

When I young, around six, I had an encounter that would shape my life far beyond anything I could have expected. I was awakened to a dark room with a desk at the end of my bed. I had spent the weekend with my aunt and knew there was no desk in that particular room. On the desk I now saw was a huge book. A gentle wind blew its leaves and made the rustling sound you might hear thumbing through the pages of an old document.

There was also a great, blinding light shining down on the book, and I remember staring at it and wondering what it all meant. I only heard these words: "This will be your call." At the voice, I became terrified and pulled the covers over my head. The next morning, I sat up quickly, but the experience had gone, and it was morning.

I have pondered that experience countless times during my life and am always amazed at how God was making my journey assured at such an early age. I do love those ancient documents that are as full of life and truth as the day they were given to their authors. God's Word is life, and I am assured of that fact.

I am grateful to Lloyd, my husband, who has supported me all our married life and, from the beginning, has never allowed me to let go of my dreams.

I am grateful to my late parents, Pastor Warren and Jean Schion, who laid a passion in me to know God, to love the Word of God and to reverence His dealings.

I am grateful to Dr. Lois Burkett, who invested in me and poured into me, when I needed skill and nurturing in my gift and calling. She walked "alongside" and "out front!"

I am grateful to the members of our beloved Abundant Life Church of Hammond,Louisiana, who helped inspire me to obey God and pursue His Word with passion.

I am grateful to Harold and Andrea McDougal, for not letting go of this project until it had come to fruition.

I am grateful to Eric Pipes and Envision Graphics for creating the cover and putting what was in my head on paper.

I am humbled for the part each of these has played in this book.

Contents

After the death of Moses the servant of the Lord, the Lord said to Joshua, son of Nun, Moses' minister, Moses My servant is dead. So now arise [take his place], go over this Jordan, you and all this people, into the land which I am giving to them, the Israelites.

Joshua 1:1-2

Introduction

In the Church today, we find ourselves in a transition period, a transition into something special that God is doing in the Spirit realm. A shift has taken place. This is important for us to realize, because if we have our eyes on the wrong things, we could miss what's about to happen.

It's possible to be right in the middle of something God is doing and still miss it. For this reason, God is calling each of us to sharpen our hearing and become alert to what He is saying and doing in the earth in this hour.

What is about to happen will affect the whole world. There is a shaking going on, and in the days to come, not even the most remote part of the earth will be left unaffected by it. God is doing a new thing, and He is inviting us to be part of it.

The days ahead are not to be, as many have suggested, a time of "doom and gloom" for the Church. They *will* mean doom and gloom (and worse) for those who don't know our God, and they may also be a time of doom and gloom for people who just play church. But for those of us who actually make up the true Church, these coming days will be glorious ones, days that we should all look forward to and eagerly embrace.

It's time to remove anything and everything that has prevented us from crossing over into all that God has for us, time for some serious soul searching. Come with me, as we learn what some of those impediments are and how to remove them. Together, we're about to cross over.

Our text for this message is found in Joshua. I always find it so interesting that the Old Testament is full of New Testament principles. Every time I read the Old Testament, I discover them there. This is especially true of the book of Joshua, as we are about to see.

As we follow the journey of the Israelites into their Promised Land, take each step by faith, and make each experience your own. It's time for *Crossing Your Jordans,* and today you can begin to possess what God has in store for YOU.

Pastor Regina Blount
Hammond, Louisiana

Part I

The New Generation

The New Opportunity

After the death of Moses the servant of the Lord, the Lord said to Joshua son of Nun, Moses' minister, Moses My servant is dead. So now arise [take his place], go over this Jordan, you and all this people, into the land which I am giving to them, the Israelites. Every place upon which the sole of your foot shall tread, this have I given to you, as I promised Moses. Joshua 1:1-3

The main elements of the message of this book are based on Joshua 5 and 6, but our journey must begin with Chapter 1. The biblical book of history known as Joshua begins with the fact that Moses had died. He had been a great leader, but that was yesterday. Now it was a new day, and yesterday was gone forever. As much as any of the people of Israel would have liked to return to their life under Moses, they could not. There was no way to recapture those days. They were gone and gone forever, and so the people had to move on.

> *This is a new day, with new challenges and new opportunities!*

Why do we always want to go back to our yesterdays? They're over, and there's nothing we should long for or desire from them. It no longer matters what we went through way back when, how or why we went through it, or even who went through it with us. That's all in the past, and this is a new day, with new challenges and new opportunities. This is, in fact, a day like no other. Don't miss it because of longing for your yesterdays.

The fact that it was a new day for the children of Israel was not something to lament. To the contrary.

In past years, they had gone round and round in the wilderness, with little or nothing to show for their efforts. Now God would purpose their steps and guide them in the way they were going. For too long they had been walking blindly, and their many steps had merely taken them in circles. Now they had a specific destination, a specific destiny. From this day on, their feet would tread with purpose or, we could say, with possession.

Having Possessing Feet

All those years of walking had not gotten the people any closer to their Promised Land. Physically, they had come very close to it, but they had failed to cross over the last barrier, the Jordan river, and to take possession of the land. Now it was a new day. Yesterday was gone, Moses was dead, and they would now walk in purpose.

Until that moment, they had walked and walked and walked and walked some more, seemingly accomplishing little or nothing in the process. Now their every step would be with purpose, and that purpose was to have a possession.

This is a message for the Church today, and it is like a fire in my bones. God is saying to us that we must no longer walk in circles. It's time to cross over and possess the land. It's time to lay hold of every promise God has given us. Without laying hold of it, you can't possess it.

This was a very big deal for the children of Israel. For forty long years they had wandered in the wilderness void of purpose. They had gained nothing for all of their efforts, for they had been walking in circles. What a tragedy! Let's you and I determine that this same fate will not befall us. It's time to cross over, and we must do whatever is necessary to make it happen.

Spying Out the Land

Joshua 2 begins with the good news that the people had now been given a new opportunity, a second chance to possess the land promised to their forefathers, and it tells us what they began to do in response:

> *Joshua the son of Nun sent two men secretly from Shittim as scouts, saying, Go, view the land, especially Jericho. And they went and came to the house of a harlot named Rahab and lodged there.*
> Joshua 2:1

In Moses' time, twelve men had been sent to spy out the land of Canaan, but what they saw there was discouraging to the majority of them. Two of the twelve, Joshua and Caleb, had come back with a good report: the land was just as good as God had said it was. But the other ten could think only of the giants they saw in the land. To make the land theirs, they would have to face those giants in battle, and they were afraid of that prospect. Because the skeptics numbered ten and those of the good report were only two, the nay-sayers won the day, and the people of Israel continued to wander in the wilderness.

Now Joshua was ready to send out spies of his own. And what would be different this time? When it came his turn to send spies, Joshua exercised extreme wisdom. Rather than send twelve men to spy out the land, as Moses had done before him, Joshua chose only two trusted aids and sent them out. He knew that he could not count on the spirituality of the majority, and for him, the opinion of two good men was more than enough.

A Powerful Conversion

Strangely, Joshua's two spies went straight to the house of a woman of ill repute, a harlot. This speaks volumes about the spiritual condition of the people of Israel as a whole as they wandered in the wilderness. They were the people of God and had a covenant with Him. Still, in general, they seemed to be absolutely clueless about what exactly their covenant with God meant. Rather than possess what was theirs as God's children, they continued to wander in circles in a barren land. A whole generation of people actually died in those desert places, when, all the while, the Promised Land awaited nearby. How sad! Now the first thing these spies did was approach a harlot.

The harlot, who's name was Rahab, represented conversion. She may have been a call girl, but at some point, she became converted. How do we know that? Because when she heard about the God of Israel and His exploits, she believed that word and obeyed it. And that's exactly how we can know that we, too, have been changed. It's not enough to simply hear God's Word. We need to hear it, but that's just a first step. After we've heard it, then we need to do it, to act on it.

Rahab was a shining example of what God was about to do for all of Israel, and they had to receive this example from a woman of ill repute. God wanted His people to hear Him and to obey Him, just as Rahab was doing. God has not called His people to be questioners, doubters, fussers and complainers. When He speaks, He desires that His people respond to Him quickly, willingly and exactly.

Hear God's words, and then get up and do what He has said. That's what pleases Him. If a call girl could be converted and begin to trust God and His Word, then you can too.

The call girl became the converted girl, and then the converted girl became the completed girl. Why do I say that? Because Rahab now labored for the Lord and won the lost. When the spies asked her what they could do in return for the kindness she showed them by hiding them in her home, she asked that her entire family be spared when they returned. And they were.

The Past Is Past

On the other side of the Jordan, the older generation was dying off, a new generation was coming on, and every one of the people was now offered a part in a new inheritance. This tells us something very important. God is not nearly as interested in your past as He is in your present and your future.

As a servant of Christ, I don't really care what you did in the past. The past is done and gone, and it should be forgotten. You have a new life before you. I'm interested in your decision for Christ today and tomorrow. If Rahab could be saved, then you can be saved too.

> *Rahab was a shining example of what God was about to do for all of Israel!*

Rahab's payoff was eternal. She found a new freedom, a new family and a new fame. What do I mean by that? She became the great-great-grandmother of King David and his honored line and was memorialized in the Bible and in Jewish history. If God would do that for a harlot, think of what He has in store for you and for me.

Getting Ready to Go In and Possess What Is Yours

By Joshua 3, the people and their leader had prepared themselves to go in and take possession of the land, and then God began to give them specific instructions about their first hurdle—the crossing of the Jordan River:

> *Yet a space must be kept between you and it [the ark], about 2000 cubits by measure; come not near it, that you may [be able to see the ark and] know the way you must go, for you have not passed this way before.* Joshua 3:4

God was giving the feet of His people direction and assuring them that, despite the fact that they had fled from the giants of the land of Canaan years before, this time they could take possession of what was rightfully theirs. To achieve it, of course, they would have to listen to Him, and they would have to obey Him. They could not fight the giants in their own strength and hope to win. But first things first. First, they had to get across the Jordan.

Defining Jordan

For the Israelites of Joshua's day, crossing the Jordan was no easy feat, and before we go any further, we need to define what the name Jordan actually means. Jordan means "a descending place." This is further clarified in the book of Jeremiah, where God said to the prophet:

> *Arise and go down to the potter's house, and there I will cause you to hear My words. Then I went down to the potter's house, and behold, he was working at the wheel.* Jeremiah 18:2-3

It was to Jordan that the young prophet was being called on this occasion, signifying that we have to go down before we can go up. Jeremiah had to be willing to be bent by God so that he could be repositioned. It is in the depths of every new Jordan in our lives that we can experience God in new ways and rise to new opportunities. In order to embrace the new, we must face the present obstacle before us and overcome it with the help of the Lord. The current challenge before us, then, represents the hope of a better tomorrow. And there are, of course, many more than one Jordans in our lives. It's more like one every day.

In Joshua's day, crossing Jordan was a very great challenge, and today it still represents exactly where most of us are in our experience with God. Therefore what God told Joshua and his people to do on this occasion is important to us. We need to know exactly what He told them to do, and then we need to do the same things they did.

Every individual had to keep his or her eyes on God in order to know His movements!

Keeping Your Eyes on God

So what did God tell the Israelites to do so that they could possess what was rightfully theirs? His first instruction to the people as they prepared to go in and take possession of the land was to keep their eyes on Him. His presence among them was represented by the Ark of the Covenant, and they were not to lose sight of it at any moment. This was not the only time He instructed them to keep their eyes fastened on Him. He told them this seven times. What does that fact show us? It shows how very important the order was. If you don't keep your eyes on Jesus, you're doomed to fail. There is no substitute for keeping your eyes fastened on Him, for He is your very life.

Too many of us in this modern world have our eyes glued to the news of the day, and we're all too often moved by what we hear or read. The problem is that our news coverage is conveyed to us by mortal men and women, and so it contains error, wrong opinions and interpretations. Even worse, it sometimes contains outright lies and deceptions. The news is not always accurate; many times it is blatantly inaccurate.

In many foreign countries, the reliability of the news media is even worse than it is here in America. Wherever they are, newsmen and women have an agenda, they represent someone, and what they say is often tinged by these realities.

So keep your eyes on God. Keep your eyes on His covenant. Keep your eyes on His glory and His majesty. If you can do that, you will not go astray.

Moving with God's Presence

There was another reason the people needed to keep the Ark of the Covenant in sight. God used it as a means of guiding them. When it moved, they were to move with it, and when it rested, they were to rest with it. This was for their safety and assurance, but it was also to keep them in the right way.

When the Ark had stopped, no man or woman could continue to move and expect to be blessed, and when the Ark began to move, no man or woman could hang back and still expect to possess what was promised. Every individual had to keep his or her eyes on God in order to know His movements, for His movements must determine their own movements—if they expected to have His favor upon their lives.

Most of us have gotten ourselves into trouble at one point or another by trying to help God. One biblical example is compelling. At a later time, when King David was taking the Ark, newly retrieved from God's enemies, back into the city of Jerusalem, the ox cart it was loaded on hit a rut, and the Ark seemed in danger of falling. A young man named Uzziah saw what was happening and reached his hand out to steady the Ark. When he did that, he was struck dead by God. What does this mean? It means that God doesn't need our help. Stop trying to help Him and surrender to His will for the moment.

At times, when the Ark began to move, I'm sure that it might not have seemed like a convenient time for some of the people to follow. I'm sure that some of them grew attached to the place they were at that moment and didn't want to leave it and that others grew attached to things they could not take on the journey and were hesitant to leave them behind. But if we are to cross over into full possession, we must be willing to physically leave the place we are and to leave the things we have and to follow after God. Go after Him—whatever the cost to you. That's an important secret for crossing over. If need be, leave whatever you have grown to love, to go after Him. You'll never be sorry. In Him is the fullness of everything you need.

Honoring God in All Things

There is a price to be paid if we want to live a life that honors God and brings Him pleasure. When the children of Israel marched toward the Promised Land, they were commanded to maintain a certain distance between themselves and the Ark. It was a holy object, one that the priests could touch, but the average person could not. Maintaining their distance from it showed a healthy respect.

Please don't dishonor the presence of God. Don't ever make light of His presence, even His presence within *you*. Don't ever make light of where God has brought you from and what He has brought you out of. Don't make light of how He has chosen to manifest His presence in your life. And God forbid that we should touch anything that would cause a mixture in our lives of the holy and the profane.

This is the challenge we're all facing today in this twenty-first century—in our homes, in our work places, and even in our churches. It's a challenge we face in our marital relationships and in our relationships with our children, our friends and our co-workers.

You face this challenge every day. Where do you go? What do you participate in? What do your ears hear? What do your eyes see? This is a constant struggle, because we're surrounded by a hostile world, and Satan wants to destroy each of us. Keep your eyes on God, move when He moves, and be careful to honor Him in all things.

Not Always Looking to Other People

Are you looking to other people for your guidance today? This is dangerous—even, at times when you're looking to "Church" leadership for your cues. Men are prone to error, so it's always best to follow God.

The same Holy Ghost who lives in me lives in you, so rise above the childlike position of always depending on others for your spiritual guidance. Set your sights on God and don't look away for a moment. Turn your face toward Him, watch Him, follow Him and honor Him, and you'll be ready to cross over into possession.

It's true that the Ark was to rest upon the shoulders of the priests, but not once did God tell the people to keep their eyes on the priests. Their future did not depend on the priests; it depended on God. Their order, therefore, was to keep their sights on Him and on no one else.

Where the Ark was going and what the Ark was doing was not the people's responsibility, so they didn't have to worry about that. Their responsibility was to obey, to keep the Ark in sight, to stop and make camp when it stopped, to break camp and follow when it moved, and to honor it in the proscribed way. Nothing more was required of them.

Let God worry about the when, the how and the why of things too deep for us to fathom. Our responsibility is but to obey Him. Only He can do the miracles. Only He can bring the conviction. Only He can heal the sick. You can't open the Red Sea, so stop trying. You can't fight giants and win, so let God do it.

The people of that older generation were also people of God!

We can take this a step further. It is God's responsibility to see that your bills get paid and that your children get saved. You do what He tells you to do, and He'll do the rest. Follow Him, keeping your eyes on Him and honoring Him as He desires, and He will never disappoint you.

A Whole New Generation

Moses was dead, and the leadership of the people now passed to Joshua, but it's important to note that this was not the same group of people Moses had led in the wilderness. This was a whole *"new generation"* (Joshua 5:2). Most of the older generation had to die off before God could permit the people to enter the land. That's one of the reasons they'd had to go round and round in the wilderness. This endless wandering had to continue until the older ones among them were all gone.

The sad thing about all of this is that the people of that older generation were also people of God, people of covenant, people of the promise. Why, then, were they not being permitted to enter the land? That's an important question, and we need some answers to it.

One answer is found way back in the writings of Moses. As Chapter 14 of the book of Numbers opens, the entire congregation of Israel is found weeping with a loud voice before God:

> *And all the congregation cried out with a loud voice, and [they] wept that night.*   Numbers 14:1

This was not just a few people weeping together. Some have estimated that Israel numbered several million people at this time. And they *"all ... cried out with a loud voice."* This went on all night long. Can you imagine what that must have been like?

What were all these people weeping about? They were weeping about the *"evil report"* brought by the spies in the previous chapter. The people had come all this way, only to be frustrated now because the land promised to them was filled with giants. This was terribly frustrating, and their protests rose up to Heaven:

> *All the Israelites grumbled and deplored their situation, accusing Moses and Aaron, to whom the whole congregation said, Would that we had died in Egypt! Or that we had died in this wilderness! Why does the Lord bring us to this land to fall by the sword? Our wives and little ones will be a prey. Is it not better for us to return to Egypt?*   Numbers 14:2-3

What were they saying? They were declaring that God was not capable of defending them against the inhabitants of Canaan. "God can't do it," they said in so many words, and they meant it. They were ready to turn back to Egypt:

> *And they said one to another, Let us choose a captain and return to Egypt.*   Numbers 14:4

This was serious, and the only thing Moses and Aaron knew to do was to cry out to God:

Then Moses and Aaron fell on their faces before all the assembly of Israelites. Numbers 14:5

How would this matter be resolved?

A Serious Offense

Others were provoked to action by this serious offense against God:

> God was angry, and He had every reason to be angry!

And Joshua son of Nun and Caleb son of Jephunneh, who were among the scouts who had searched the land, rent their clothes, and they said to all the company of Israelites, The land through which we passed as scouts is an exceedingly good land. If the Lord delights in us, then He will bring us into this land and give it to us, a land flowing with milk and honey. Only do not rebel against the Lord, neither fear the people of the land, for they are bread for us. Their defense and the shadow [of protection] is removed from over them, but the Lord is with us. Fear them not. Numbers 14:6-9

Joshua and Caleb were the two spies who had given the good report, and now they were understandably angry. After all that God had done for these people, how could they act like He had never shown up for them at all? This was too much to bear! No wonder God was so offended by the attitude of these people! They were ungrateful complainers.

The rending of one's clothes in Old Testament times, as Joshua and Caleb performed it here, was reserved for the most serious of circumstances. In fact, this ceremonial act was usually only carried out when someone important had died. The actions of Joshua and Caleb show us that murmuring is a very deadly and serious matter.

"Why can't God give us the land?" these two men insisted. "If He delights in us," then this land *will* be ours." And they proceeded to describe it again as God had, *"a land flowing with milk and honey."* A land like that would be a whole lot better than the people had at the moment. It would be, in fact, better than anything they had ever experienced in their lifetime.

Two Men Stood Firm

The Israelites were rebelling against the Lord because they feared the people of the land, but at least two men were not afraid at all. *"They are bread for us,"* Joshua and Caleb declared. How could they say that? Because they knew that God had *"removed"* the defenses of the enemy. These enemies had no covenant with God, but Israel did. *"The Lord is with us,"* Joshua and Caleb declared, and the logical conclusion was: *"Fear them not."*

This did not elicit the response the two men of faith had hoped for:

> *But all the congregation said to stone [Joshua and Caleb] with stones.* Numbers 14:10

It was only a direct intervention by the Lord that saved these two faithful leaders that day:

> *But the glory of the Lord appeared at the Tent of Meeting before all the Israelites.*
>   Numbers 14:10

God was angry, and He had every reason to be angry. His anger was expressed to Moses:

> *And the Lord said to Moses, How long will this people provoke (spurn, despise) Me? And how long will it be before they believe Me [trusting in, relying on, clinging to Me], for all the signs which I have performed among them?*
>   Numbers 14:11

That's exactly what you do when you murmur against God. You're spurning Him and despising

Him, and that's a very difficult thing for God to bear. Nothing could be more insulting to Him. Your actions and your attitude show that you're failing to believe Him. As the Amplified Bible shows us, this means that you're not trusting in Him, relying on Him or clinging to Him. And you're doing this, despite everything God has done for you in the past. That's hard to understand. No wonder God is angered!

The People of Promise Failed to Receive the Promise

These people of promise failed to receive the promise because of their insufferable murmuring and complaining. They may have been churchgoers, and apparently they were. But that didn't matter. Their complaining would keep them out of the Promised Land.

The Israelites may have been tithers, and apparently they were. But that didn't matter. Their complaining would keep them out of the Promised Land.

They may have been able to quote the Scriptures, and apparently they could. But that didn't matter. Their complaining would now keep them out of the Promised Land.

It is important for us to learn all that we can about this sin of murmuring that prevented the older generation of the children of Israel from partaking of the new thing. I'm convinced that this is the very thing that often keeps the heavens closed over many of us.

Murmuring Is Deadly

When God spoke to me to preach on this subject, I thought I knew what murmuring was, but, then, when I began to examine the Scriptures concerning this subject, I quickly saw that there was much more to murmuring than I had previously realized. May God help us to learn to avoid this deadly sin.

Murmuring often comes from the lips, but it's possible to murmur with your heart and never actually speak a word out loud. If you're thinking it, that's the same as saying it. If it's in your heart, then it's real.

Murmuring means "to stop, to stay permanently, to be abstinent, especially to complain, a continuous sound like a stream, to be discontented." *Webster's* calls it "not a normal sound (i.e. a heart murmur)." Murmur means "to believe a lie and lodge a lie there, to hold a grudge and remain there, to grumble, to complain, to whisper, as with a thought." By any definition, murmuring is a very serious offense against God.

These people had an inheritance, something that had been prepared for them from the beginning of time, and the principle thing that kept them from it was their murmuring. God had brought them out of bondage to bring them into their Promised Land, but the thing that prevented them from reaching it and kept them lingering in some lesser circumstance was their perpetual murmuring. Clearly, murmuring is a deadly sin.

How can a man or woman of God ever murmur against Him when He has done so much for each of us? It's because we have the tendency to forget the miracles He has done, what He's brought us through, and this prevents us from being able to look forward to what He will now do today and in the days to come.

> *We murmur about so many things!*

God is dealing with us on this subject. We want His blessings, but what kind of conduct are we engaged in at the moment? An open heaven is your portion, but murmuring can close it in a second.

Are you constantly griping about your circumstances in life? What is it today? The floor? The walls? Your spouse? Your children? Your clothes? Your job? What you don't have and you want so badly? Every time you complain in this way, what you're actually saying is this: "God can't change my circumstances.

He's powerless to make a difference in my daily life." And that's a very serious charge. No wonder God's offended by that! He's so offended that He closes His windows over your life.

When you're making statements that seem to indicate that God's not big enough for the situation of the moment, you're as bad or worse than the Israelites who were badmouthing God in the wilderness. And, if this is true, what can you expect from Him?

Modern-day Christians Are Also Guilty of Murmuring

It's utterly amazing how we Christians murmur today—even about our church activities. We murmur because we don't have enough clothes to wear or they're not clean or properly pressed. We murmur because we're always too rushed to get ready and get to the church on time. We murmur because it's too hot (or too cold) in the sanctuary. We murmur because the service is too long (or too short). We murmur because of something the preacher said or didn't say that day.

We murmur about our vehicles (they're not as nice as the latest thing on the market), about our houses (they always require some maintenance or upgrade) and about our paychecks (they never seem to go far enough). We murmur about so many things, and the reason we vocalize it is that our minds have been captivated by it.

The wise Solomon said:

A [self-confident] fool utters all of his anger, but a wise man holds it back and stills it.

Proverbs 29:11

I love that verse because it's so true. Too many of us give voice to everything that flits through our minds, and much of it is not worth the effort it takes to put it into words.

With others, they don't have to say a thing. You know what they're thinking. You can be on the other side of the room, and you know. They don't have to open their mouth. The look on their face says it all.

This Is Even More Important Today

Today our attitude toward God is more important than ever. In the New Testament, God no longer looks at our exterior. He's not interested in the length of your hair, and He's not offended when women wear pants. He looks past the outer veneer of a person, the part that will one day wrinkle and die. Instead, He looks at the inner person, that part of a person that is eternal. That inner person, and that alone, is what

God judges you by, and if it's filled with murmuring and complaining, what can God think?

God's Will Was Thwarted

God, our heavenly Father, delights in blessing His children. He wanted to give this land to the children of Israel, and He had promised it to them. But He could not tolerate one more insult from their heart and lips. That was all the murmuring and complaining He could bear.

> *God was making a formal oath before the Israelites that day!*

When Joshua and Caleb were bold enough to speak up against the injustice being perpetuated by the people, those who heard them didn't humble themselves and repent. Instead, they wanted to stone the two men who had told them the truth. And God could not tolerate that affront. He stepped in personally and prevented it.

Can you imagine the nerve these people had? Someone tells them the truth about their attitude and actions, and they want to stone them. That was more than God could tolerate. These men would not possess His land. That was final!

God Will Only Tolerate So Much

This is an important New Testament truth concealed in an Old Testament passage. Paul, for instance, had much to say about murmuring and complaining. He showed us that God simply won't tolerate it:

We should not tempt the Lord [try His patience, become a trial to Him, critically appraise Him, and exploit His goodness] as some of them did—and were killed by poisonous serpents; nor discontentedly complain as some of them did—and were put out of the way entirely by the destroyer (death).
1 Corinthians 10:9-10

"We should not!" What more need be said?

Jude spoke of judgment against those who resist God:

Behold, the Lord comes with His myriads of holy ones ... to execute judgment upon all and to convict all the impious (unholy ones) and all of their ungodly deeds which they have committed [in such an] ungodly [way], and of all the severe (abusive, jarring) things which ungodly sinners have spoken against Him. Jude 1:14-15

Who were these people who had so offended God? He tells us in the very next verse:

These are inveterate murmurers (grumblers) who complain [of their lot in life]. Jude 1:16

Nothing could be more clear. So be forewarned, friend. You can't murmur and be blessed. Murmuring will close Heaven over you faster than anything else. If murmuring kept an entire generation of the children of Israel out to of the Promised Land, who are you to do it and prosper today?

Another Deadly Sin

Joshua 5 adds another element to the reasons behind the failure of this older generation to go in and possess the land:

For the Israelites walked forty years in the wilderness till all who were men of war who came out of Egypt perished, because they did not hearken to the voice of the Lord; to them the Lord swore that He would not let them see the land which the Lord swore to their fathers to give us, a land flowing with milk and honey. Joshua 5:6

Something happened that caused the Lord to go back on His word. He had sworn to Abraham, Isaac and Jacob, and again to the Israelites in Egypt that He would give them the land of Canaan. Now, He swore again, and what He swore this time was just the opposite as what He had sworn before. Not only would He *not* give them the land as He had promised; He wouldn't even let them *"see the land"* because their attitude had so angered Him.

What does it mean when it says that God *"swore"*? This is not the swearing we think of when someone takes the name of the Lord in vain. Rather, it is somewhat like the oath taken before a court of law. God was making a formal oath before the Israelites that day. This was a deadly serious matter.

A Powerful Oath

The original language used here, however, reveals that this was more than a usual oath. This type of oath was considered to be seven times more powerful than normal oaths. This was about as emphatic as anyone could get. God was making an important statement, and He wanted everyone to know the power of it, so He said it in this dramatic way. These men would not inherit the land He had promised to their fathers, and He swore it in an oath seven times more powerful than normal. They had offended Him too much.

These were the Israelites in the wilderness, and the reason they were often called *"the children of Israel"* may have been that they were such children. They acted just like a bunch of spoiled brats ... until God had finally "had it" with them. He had sworn to their fathers that this land would be theirs, but now something was forcing His hand to change that original declaration. It had been made with an oath, but now, as much as He hated it, He had to go back on His word. The words and actions of these people had driven Him to this point. He now made a more forceful oath, and with it revoked the first oath. They could not have the land. And that was final!

It Would Take a New Generation

The men and women of the older generation were still called the children of Israel, and they looked and acted very much like the children of Israel, but they would now wander in the wilderness until they died. They would never possess the land reserved for them for generations. It would take a new breed of Israelite to cross over and possess it, a totally new generation.

There would be a measure of blessing upon the older generation, and they would see some miracles at the hand of God, but the ultimate blessing, the best of the best, would never be theirs. They had forfeited it.

Disobedience Is Deadly

So what was this second deadly sin that kept the people out of the land? The previous generation must die, God said, *"because they did not hearken to the voice of the Lord."* How much plainer could we ask the Word of God to be? We know exactly why they died. *"Because they did not hearken to the voice of the Lord."* That's a very serious indictment!

To *hearken* means "to obey." The fact that they did not hearken to the voice of the Lord means that they did not obey Him. They heard what He said, but they didn't hear it with a willing heart. If they had, they would have obeyed. This is an important key for us all in our everyday walk with God.

Unfortunately, the Bible is not filled with pictures, but it does paint pictures for us with words, and this

> *They acted just like a bunch of spoiled brats ... until God had finally "had it" with them!*

is a powerful word picture. In the Bible, every word counts, and the pictures painted by the fullness of the words counts. This particular picture is one that we should all heed.

This is very specific: *"They did not hearken to the voice of the Lord."* All of their wanderings, their ordeal of spending forty years in the wilderness, their missing out on the best of the best in their lives had one specific cause. It was all due to the simple fact that *"they did not hearken to the voice of the Lord."*

"They did not." They did not what? They did not hearken. To *hearken* also means "to hear intelligently, to hear with consent, to hear with extra diligence." In other words, it means "to listen carefully, with the intent to carry out what is being ordered."

To *hearken* means "to perceive what is being said, to proclaim what is being said, and to obey what is being said." It's never enough just to hear what God is saying. His words always demand action on our part. It's never enough just to have spiritual perception and understand what God is saying. It's also never enough just to be willing to proclaim what God is saying. Our obligation to God is complete only when we have perceived, proclaimed and then obeyed what He has shown us.

This is the reason God termed the report delivered by ten of the returning spies of Moses' era to be *"an evil report."* Their words were deadly because they contradicted what God had said. These men were proclaiming what they had perceived with their natural senses, not what God was saying. Their perceptions were directly opposed to what God had said.

So, the sins that kept the people out of the land were that of murmuring and disobedience. The two go together, and they feed on each other. Therefore, we must avoid them at all costs if we are to cross over and possess all that is ours in the days ahead.

A New Style of Warfare

There may be a third reason for the failure of the former generation to enter into the land. The Scriptures state that everyone who had knowledge from previous wars (meaning all who walked in their own understanding and ability) died on the other side of the Jordan. They understood only old methods of warfare.

The Israelites had learned to fight as they were confronted by enemies along the way from Egypt, but what God was about to do was so radical that His people would have to forget all the old methods of warfare and learn a whole new strategy. (More on this later.) Suffice it to say here that it was a new day, and only those who understood the new day and flowed with it could participate.

Not Everyone Failed

As we have noted, not every individual in the older generation failed God. Joshua and Caleb, at least, did not. Joshua now received the call to lead the new generation, and, as we will see in a later chapter, Caleb became a possessor in the new land. Through their obedience, these two men escaped death and became part of a new order of things, a new opportunity for a new generation.

CHAPTER 2

The New Circumcision

So it was their uncircumcised children whom He raised up in their stead whom Joshua circumcised, because the rite had not been performed on the way. Joshua 5:7

It Was Time for Circumcision

We'll deal with the actual crossing of the Jordan in Part II of the book. For the moment, let's look ahead at some of the other new things required for this new generation if they were to possess all that was rightfully theirs. Although they had now crossed that first seemingly impenetrable barrier, there were some more things they needed to do to get ready for actual possession. Now God gave them the first one:

> *At that time the Lord said to Joshua, Make knives of flint and circumcise the [new generation of] Israelites as before. So Joshua made knives of flint and circumcised the sons of Israel at Gibeath-haaraloth. And this is the reason Joshua circumcised them: all the males of the people who came out of Egypt, all the men of war, had died in the wilderness on the way after they came out of Egypt. Though all the people who came out were circumcised, yet all the people who were born in the wilderness on the way after Israel came out of Egypt had not been circumcised.* Joshua 5:3-5

God told Joshua to circumcise this *"new generation."* But why? *"And this is the reason... ."* There was a reason for circumcising the new generation, and the reason God gave them was simple. The former generation had been circumcised, but the new generation had not.

The former generation had now walked in the wilderness for forty years because of their unbelief, their disobedience and their complaining. They had been circumcised, they had been delivered from Egypt, and they had taught themselves to war with the express purpose of going back to take possession of the Promised Land. But they'd never gotten there. *"They did not hearken to the voice of the Lord,"* and they angered God with their constant complaining, and these failures proved to be fatal.

> *There were some more things they needed to do to get ready for actual possession!*

All these years, the land of Canaan had been there waiting for them. It was, God said, theirs for the taking. It was a wonderful land, one that He described as *"flowing with milk and honey."* It had been promised to them, and yet they had never laid hold of it. Now their uncircumcised children would be raised up and allowed to enter the land instead.

Why Had Circumcision Been Neglected?

It may be understandable that the rite of circumcision was not performed during the flight from Egypt, but why had it not been done in the intervening years in the wilderness? This was the rite that set the people of Israel apart from all others. Circumcision was a symbol of their unique covenant with God. They needed to be circumcised. They needed to maintain covenant with God. The new generation would be allowed to go into the land to possess it, but not without circumcision.

Circumcision was not a cure-all. The older generation had been circumcised, so they *were* covenant people. As covenant people, they were convinced that they would ultimately have all the blessings coming to them. Still, they missed their day of crossing over and their day of possession.

We've already seen some of the reasons, but why would men of the covenant murmur and become stubborn and rebellious? I'm convinced that it all stemmed from a lack of desire on their part. They had never tasted milk and honey, and their appetites were still trained for the garlic, cucumbers and melons of Egypt. In all their years of wandering, they never developed a taste for the good things of God. Consequently, God had to write off an entire generation. It had been a generation of promise, but the men of that generation had failed to honor Him, so the promise went unfulfilled.

The older generation had an old mindset, they were stubborn and set in their ways, and they refused to bend their will to God's will. They refused to look to God, to trust Him, and to honor Him. Faithfulness was (and still is) as important as believing. God let an entire generation die off in the wilderness without ever possessing to show us just how important.

We Need Some Cutting

God said this new generation had to be circumcised, and so Joshua circumcised them. We all need some cutting off of the old so that we can embrace the new. It may be painful, but welcome it. It will set you apart from all others.

The people God was allowing to cross over and posses the land were of a turned mind. They had been circumcised, and their old shame had been removed. In fact, everything old had been removed from them. You and I need just such a radical renewal today.

May God help us to get rid of our judgmental attitudes. May the Lord forgive us because, all too often, we rise in judgment against others. In those moments, we take off the robes of righteousness He has so graciously placed on us, and we put on the robes of a judge. This is dangerous because God has declared that such judgment is His right alone:

Beloved, never avenge yourselves, but leave the way open for [God's] wrath; for it is written, Vengeance is Mine, I will repay [requite], says the Lord. Romans 12:19

> If our fruit is not right, then we're not right!

When we put on the robe of a judge, we close the heavens over ourselves, and the reason is that we're not called to be judges. God is the Judge, and when we try to do His work, the heavens close over us, and we're no longer the beloved son in whom He is well pleased. Forgive us, Lord.

There are many things that God wants to cut off of our lives, and the ideal we're working toward is to be like Him. We have a long way to go, don't we?

In our Abundant Life Church in Hammond, Louisiana, we conduct what we call our Solid Rock Classes, in which we lay a foundation for our people (particularly our leaders) in what we believe as Christians. But a class like that is only the beginning.

Each of us needs to work on our behavior daily so that we can become what God intends us to be.

Too many Christians are caught in cycles of destructive behavior. Behavioral problems are not reserved for sinners. Many Christians, although they should be seated in heavenly places, are acting like idiots or juveniles when it comes to day-to-day living. Get them outside the church, perhaps at a red light, standing in a long line, or when their paycheck comes late for some reason, and you'll quickly see what they're really like.

Do something that gets them angry, let them hear that someone has said something about them that's not true, or agitate them in some other way, and suddenly you'll find another type of fruit entirely coming forth from their lives. If this is true of us, then we need some behavior adjustment. If our fruit is not right, then we're not right.

If we're seated in heavenly places, then it's time to bring up the level of our daily behavior to match our position. Whether you like it or not, your fruit will be picked and examined, and it's time to make it what it should be.

What It Meant to Be a New Generation

All of the old must be cut away, God showed Joshua, even the negative generational influences.

This new generation could no longer afford to emulate Mama or Daddy. Mama and Daddy were being left behind. The new generation had to be what God was calling *them* to be.

It wasn't good enough to be like Grandma or Pawpaw. Only a new generation could go into the land. This generation was not to model itself after the old. It was to be something no one had ever seen before. This generation was to be made up of a rare breed. This is consistent with other Bible teachings:

Who gave Himself on our behalf that He might redeem us (purchase our freedom) from all iniquity and purity for Himself a people [to be peculiarly His own, people who are] eager and enthusiastic about [living a life that is good and filled with] beneficial deeds.   Titus 2:14

But you are a chosen race, a royal priesthood, a dedicated nation, [God's] own purchased, special people, that you may set forth the wonderful deeds and display the virtues and perfections of Him Who called you out of darkness into His marvelous light.   1 Peter 2:9

You cannot afford to be a carbon copy of anyone but God, so cut off anything and everything that opposes Him.

Your parents may have been wonderful people, but some of the things they taught you may now have to be abandoned. As much as you love them, cut off anything that may hinder you from entering into the new.

Actually three things took place there in the tent of meeting as the people prepared themselves to possess the land: (1) The cutting away or circumcision, (2) The bleeding that resulted from that cutting away, and (3) The healing that was necessary before they could move on.

Part of the ceremony of circumcision was the necessary shedding of blood. Since every male was cut and had to shed his blood, each one received this personal reminder of the importance of a sacrifice being made in his stead. As Christians, we now have the New Testament truth:

Without the shedding of blood *there is neither release from sin and its guilt nor the remission of the due and merited punishment for sins.*
Hebrews 9:22

And, of course, Jesus was the sacrificial Lamb who took our place and shed His blood so that we would hot have to shed ours. It is imperative that we keep His blood applied to our hearts continually. How foolish it is of us to trample His blood by allowing things to remain in our hearts that don't please God. He wants to cut all of them off from us, and we should want them cut off as well. We cannot afford to allow anything at all to hinder us in our relationship with God.

A Defenseless Generation

At this point, the men of the new generation, recently circumcised, found themselves in enemy territory, incapable of defending themselves should they be attacked. All they could do was remain in their tents until they were healed. Even in this, God was proving a point to His people. He would be their defense.

In every way, God was revealing Himself to a new generation, one that would understand who and what He was. And it was in that revelation that they would become possessors of the land.

The very thing that prepared the children of Israel for conquest made them vulnerable to the enemy. God did it this way to prove to them that He was able to care for them, even when they were vulnerable to attack and felt personally defenseless.

Get Healed

Joshua 5:8 contains a good word for the Church today:

When they finished circumcising all the males of the nation, they remained in their places in the camp till they were healed.

Joshua 5:8

Cut off the old, but then get healed before you try to go out and attack any enemies.

Cut off the past. Cut off what holds you back. Cut off your yesterdays. Cut off what has brought you sadness and strife. Cut off whatever is hindering you. But then, whatever you do, wait for your healing before you attempt to proceed.

It doesn't seem reasonable, but remain in your tent until you are healed. Get over the past, so that you can move on with the future. Get healed—whatever that takes. After you get rid of all your "stuff," take time to be healed so that you can be strong enough to begin to take enemy territory.

> *I'd rather have God's favor any day than rejoice in old customs and traditions!*

Don't just sit around and die from the wounds of circumcision, the cutting off of religious traditions and personal and family traits that hinder. Let's face it. This is a painful process, and you have to recover from it and move on.

Is it worth the pain? Absolutely. If something, anything, will keep you from God's very best, then willingly and gladly let it be cut off of you. It's not worth hanging on to. I'd rather have God's favor any day than rejoice in old customs and traditions. What's difficult about that choice?

Personally, I'd leave in a heartbeat anything I knew was keeping me from God's best, and I would never go back to it. After all, I have nothing to lose and everything to gain. For any of us, that should be a very easy decision to make.

After the cutting comes the healing process. You can't carry this wound with you forever. Get healed, so that you can move on.

The Rolling Away of Reproach

Don't hesitate to cut off the old. It will prevent you from entering and possessing. The cutting off is the rolling away of reproach:

And the Lord said to Joshua, This day have I rolled away the reproach of Egypt from you. So the name of the place is called Gilgal to this day. Joshua 5:9

"This day!" On *this day,* God had rolled away their reproach! When does He do it? Today. *This day!*

The cutting off of the exterior was all about rolling away reproach. What has brought shame to your life in the past? What has brought you embarrassment? What has hurt you? What has brought you pain and discouragement? It's time to roll it all away. This is your day for deliverance.

Because of what was done in that place, from that day onward it was known as Gilgal, which means "the place of the rolling off." Where is your Gilgal today?

Twice before this the children of Israel had been called a reproach to God. The first time was when Moses had come down from Mount Sinai and found the people inebriated and worshiping a golden calf (see Exodus 32:1-2). That was a such a reproach to God that three thousand men died because of it.

Do Christians today worship other gods? Oh yes! Many do.

The second case in which the children of Israel had been a reproach is found in Numbers 14:11. There the people refused to go into the land because they had seen the giants who currently occupied it, and God called that action a reproach. The God of the Universe had said that they could possess the land, but they had decided otherwise. What idiots! What a reproach to His name!

Those two reproaches, the things that had kept their forefathers from entering in and possessing the land, along with every other reproach, were now being rolled away. God was cutting off all their reproach, and it would never be thrown up in their faces again.

> *Joshua and the new generation were to receive double what was promised in the original covenant!*

The reproaches of the past could not keep God's new generation from the things He was now bringing them into. There isn't a devil big enough to keep God from being God, and there's not a past or a failure big enough to prevent Him from fulfilling His Word.

God could have ordered this rite of circumcision to be performed before they ever got to the Jordan, but He did it this way to prove to them that He was God. Within sight of their enemies, they would cut off the old and find a new beginning.

Covenant Is Our Identity

In order to cross over and begin to possess the land, you have to understand that it's all wrapped up in who you are in God. You can cross over only because of the covenant you have with Him, not for any other reason. So if you're unable to understand your covenant (represented by circumcision), you can never cross over.

When many of us were growing up in Sunday school and church, it seemed to us that inheriting in God was simply a matter of being born into the right family. Isaac couldn't lose because he had the right parents—Abraham and Sarah. But it doesn't work that way at all. Each individual must make effective his or her own covenant agreement with God. Much of the blessings promised to Abraham were lost until Jesus came to earth and redeemed mankind. Now I can have that blessing, although I may not be technically a daughter of Abraham. If I follow God in faith, I am the spiritual seed of Abraham.

The important point is that I must be obedient to God today. Nothing in the past guarantees my blessing.

"As Before"?

There is an important phrase in Joshua 5:2 that we want to understand. Let's look at it again:

At that time the Lord said to Joshua, Make knives of flint and circumcise the [new generation of] Israelites as before. Joshua 5:2

"As before." What did that mean? When studying this portion of scripture one day, I was lead to read this phrase over and over, and I sensed that I was not fully understanding what God was saying. What did He mean by *"as before"*? Were the Israelites just going back to the same thing they'd had before? Surely not.

The King James Version of the Bible uses the phrase *"the second time."* That didn't seem to help me much either.

I looked up this phrase and found that it meant "to be totally converted, to be totally delivered, to be fetched home again, to call to mind, to get oneself back again, extra recovery, extra recompense, extra relief, extra rescue, extra restoration, extra return, extra reverse, extra reward, and extra take back." It also meant "extra withdrawal."

In other words, Joshua and the new generation were to receive double what was promised in the original covenant. They were not just returning to something already experienced. Their experience would go far beyond that of the original generation. They would not only possess the *same* as the previous generation had; they would turn around and repossess it. They would possess it twice or have a double portion of it. I now understood. What they were doing was even better than before.

A Historic Day

The day of circumcision marked a new milestone for the people. *"This day"!* It was a historic occasion, a marked day, a day worth remembering. It was the day God reopened the heavens over His people. It was the day the powerful magnitude 7 oath sworn over the previous generation was broken, and the people could again have what God had promised them all along. All the reproach had been rolled off at Gilgal, and they were ready for a new day.

"This day," there is no longer any reproach on you, nothing to hold you back. Absolutely nothing can now prevent you from taking the territory God has promised you. God has rolled away from you all that hindered. It's time for celebration:

And the Israelites encamped in Gilgal.

Joshua 5:10

They just camped there for a while. And why not? It was time to celebrate. Their reproach had been taken away. They probably sang a little song of victory:

The reproach is gone.
The reproach is gone.
We're going in now,
For the reproach is gone.

I can somehow visualize them just having themselves a time, stirring up some dust. It was a wonderful moment. Why not enjoy it!

Don't Fear God's Circumcision

So don't be afraid of God's circumcision. If He needs to circumcise your heart, let Him do it willingly and joyfully. Get in your tent, and then let Him take the sharpness of His Word, the preciseness of His wisdom and cut off everything that is religious and carnal and dead in you. Let Him cut away all murmuring, all griping and all complaining.

There are many things that you don't yet understand and many things that you need an answer to. If you will go into His holy place and lie at His feet, He will enlighten you. Tell Him, "Lord, so much of this 'stuff' is weighing me down. I don't need it, and I don't want it. Remove it from me." He'll answer that prayer.

Go into His secret place, the place of surrender, and God will rescue you. He will cover you. He will heal you. And He will never break covenant with you.

As painful as it sounds, let Him cut you. Let Him cut off all that offends. He gave His very life for you, so He's worthy of your trust. As the Master Surgeon, He can cut away from you everything that hinders, and leave you whole.

Our Lord was wounded for you. Trust Him to wound you so that you can now be healed. He suffered torture for you. Trust Him with His skillful knife. Receive the new circumcision today.

CHAPTER 3

The New Food

*And on the same day they ate the produce of
the land: unleavened cakes and parched grain.
And the manna ceased on the day after they ate
of the produce of the land: and the Israelites
had manna no more, but they ate of the fruit
of the land of Canaan that year.*

Joshua 5:11-12

The Celebration of Passover

After the Israelites had received the new circumcision, they did something else. They celebrated the Passover meal for the first time since leaving Egypt.

> No generation must be allowed to forget what God had done in Egypt!

And they kept the Passover on the fourteenth day of the month at evening in the plains of Jericho. Joshua 5:10

The Passover meal was not just to be a onetime event. God Himself instituted the meal as a means of reminding the people of His goodness. No generation must be allowed to forget what He had done in Egypt.

The fact that Joshua chose to eat this meal at this particular moment displays incredible insight on his part. Passover recalled the time when the blood had been applied to the doorposts of every home in Goshen, and, as a result, the death angel had passed over their houses and families. Now, as they were about to embark on a campaign to possess the land that was promised to them, they paused to remember what God had done for their parents and grandparents in Egypt.

The keeping of the Passover was done so that the people could remember the blood that had been applied to redeem them. And when they did, a wonderful thing happened. No sooner had they been circumcised than they were able to eat a new food.

"In the Plains of Jericho"

The Israelites celebrated Passover *"in the plains of Jericho."* Why was this fact important? They chose to camp in a place from which they could see what they intended to possess. They could see Jericho, and soon it would be theirs.

Jericho would be theirs because they had rid themselves of murmuring and complaining, and all reproach had been rolled away from them. The people were no longer divided, a few up front giving advice, while trying to ward off stones from the rest of the crowd. They were now united, having a common goal. They were in one accord about where they were going and what they intended to do there. They were happy with God, He was happy with them, and they were happy about what that meant for their future. This combination produced, for them, a new food. It was a new day, and it was to be marked by a new diet.

This new generation had a new circumcision, and with it came a new food. We, also, need to come to a higher revelation. If we're still feasting on John 3:16, or we're right where we were spiritually ten years ago, then we urgently need to grow up. The manna of the wilderness was wonderful, but God has something better for His people today.

The New Diet

We all appreciate a little variety in our diets, and the Israelites were no different. They had been eating the same thing day in and day out for forty years. As wonderful as the manna was, it must have grown to be monotonous to them. Now, it was a new day, and as a sign of new things to come, they had new things to eat.

When my husband and I travel to other countries, he wants to try all the new dishes he's offered, while I'm a lot less adventurous with my food. I've found a few things that I really enjoy, so I eat them over and over again, and because of that, I'm always eager to get home and have more variety in my diet. In the meantime, he's enjoying himself immensely. He loves all the curry dishes, even the really hot ones.

When we're on our way home from the airport, I want to stop at a Wendy's restaurant to taste some American French fries and a cold Dr. Pepper. My husband always offers to buy me a hamburger. "No thanks," I say, "but make the fries a BIG order."

Can you imagine eating the same thing for forty years? I can't.

It Wasn't God's Fault

It wasn't God's fault that the children of Israel had a monotonous diet. God gave them just what they deserved. Considering all the heartache they put Him through and all the complaining they did against Him and His servant, it's a wonder that God gave them anything to eat at all. It was only His great mercy and grace that He didn't abandon them to starve in the wilderness.

I think that by giving them the same food to eat every single day God was showing them what it was like for Him to have to listen to their constant murmuring and complaining. They had to face the same problems every day, with their flesh and mind, and with their families. And they had to go around and around. God was showing them what it was like. "Oh no! Not this again!"

Don't force God to back off from His commitment to you. He has promised you an open Heaven. Now, let Him deliver it to you. He is a God of covenant and, with Him, covenant is sacred. He never breaks covenant, but we do.

Get all of that old "stuff" cut off, and then come out healed and ready to move forward. Then, you'll get something new to eat.

They Rejoiced

Now the manna ceased, the people ate the produce of the land, and they rejoiced. Jericho was before them, and as a sign of the new things to come, God was feeding them with new things.

It might not have required much nourishment for the people to go around in circles in the wilderness, but now they needed all the nourishment they could get. They had to rally to defeat Jericho, and God now gave them unleavened cakes and parched grain.

One of the most amazing things about this new food was that the Israelites did not have to work for it. It was given to them by God. I don't know what train brought it to them (there were so many of them that they would have needed a whole trainload), but somehow it got to them just when they needed it.

This was not something the Israelites had planted, cultivated and harvested. This was part of their covenant. Through Moses, God had said:

On the day when you pass over the Jordan to the land your God gives you …

All these blessings shall come upon you and overtake you… . Blessed shall you be in the city and blessed shall you be in the field. Blessed shall be the fruit of your body and the fruit of your ground and the fruit of your beast, the increase of your cattle and the young of your flock. Blessed shall be your basket and your kneading trough. Blessed shall you be when you come in and blessed shall you be when you go out.

Deuteronomy 27:2 and 28:2-6

And it was happening.

God wants us to be blessed in all that we do, in everything we put our hands to. When you enter your place of employment, covenant and Kingdom principles should take over there. Your job, your bosses and your co-workers should be blessed just because you're there. And when you walk away, that blessing just might go with you as a sign to everyone around you that God's favor is upon your life.

The food God offered His people contained no yeast, a symbol of sin, and nothing that would cause it to be bitter. God's promise is:

As a sign of the new things to come, God was feeding them with new things!

*The blessing of the Lord—it makes [truly] rich, and
He adds no sorrow with it.*   Proverbs 9:22

What Was this Old Corn?

Most translations call these grains God gave His
people *"corn,"* but some call it *"old corn."* That didn't
make it bad. It simply meant that it was corn reserved
for a previous generation. This was the corn the Israelites had waited for for so long, and it had long been
their portion, but the older generation had never gotten there to partake of it. Now, finally, it was there for
the new generation to taste and experience. God has
been waiting on us for a long time, and He has some
corn waiting for us too—when we get ready to eat it.

What determined the food they would eat? Did
it depend on God? Or did it depend on them? When
they got in the place they needed to be and, more
importantly, in the condition they needed to be in,
the long-promised food was there for them to partake
of. So what you eat is largely determined by your attitude and actions, by your willingness to trust God
and obey Him and not simply murmur and complain
and blame Him for your own failures. Your corn is
waiting. Get to where you need to be and get your
heart circumcised so that you can finally eat what's
been waiting for you for so long now.

We have it all backwards. We want God to feed
us before we respond in the way that's pleasing to

Him. He, on the other hand, demands that we do it His way. Your corn will be reserved until you get there, so what are you waiting for?

God has a lot more than corn stored up for us. He has everything we need or want, but He's just waiting for us to get there. In the process, our heart must be in tune with our mouth, our mouth must be in tune with our heart, and our mind must be in tune with both. It's time for a new food. Come and get your portion today.

The Manna Ceased

The next day after the Israelites ate this new food, the manna suddenly ceased. Why would that happen? The manna, which literally meant "What is it?" was no longer needed. The people of Israel had received a revelation. Their eyes had been opened. Their ears had been unstopped. And they suddenly understood something their forefathers had struggled with. This new generation had the revelation: God is God, and there is no god but Him. And with that revelation came promotion and provision. So much came to them in such a short time that they no longer needed what their fathers had come to depend on for forty years. And it all happened because a new generation was receiving a new understanding of God.

This is the reason the enemy is working overtime to make people stupid about who God is. Satan doesn't want people to know the truth about this great God of ours. So he causes people to be irreverent, to use God's name in vain, to make jokes about Him and to neglect His Word.

"Stay stupid," he urges. "Catch up on your sleep during church services; you've been working very hard recently."

"Don't pay your tithes; you can't really afford it."

"Don't witness to people; they might resent it."

May God help us to listen to truth, not lies! When we know who God is, it changes everything.

> *It all happened because a new generation was receiving a new understanding of God!*

They Ate the Fruit of the Land

After they ate the new food and the manna ceased, how did they live? *"They ate of the fruit of the land."* How interesting! The Israelites hadn't had time yet to begin possessing the land, but they were already reaping the benefits of that coming possession. They hadn't had time to advise all their new neighbors that they would have to evacuate because the land they were currently occupying had been given to them by God, and yet they were already enjoying the fruits of their possession.

In the Spirit realm, God was telling them, "It's yours; you have it; you own this land; it is established; I have given it to you," and this new generation understood this revelation and began acting like they believed what God was saying for once.

This new generation, with the new opportunity had now experienced a new circumcision and had eaten a new food. What was next?

CHAPTER 4

The New Messenger

When Joshua was by Jericho, he looked up, and behold, a Man stood near him with His drawn sword in His hand. And Joshua went to Him and said to Him, Are you for us or for our adversaries?

And He said, No [neither], but as Prince of the Lord's host have I now come.

*And Joshua fell on His face to the earth and
worshipped, and said to Him, What says my
Lord to His servant?
And the Prince of the Lord's host said to
Joshua, Loose your shoes from off your feet, for
the place where you stand is holy. And Joshua
did so.*   Joshua 5:13-15

The Messenger

For this new generation with a new opportunity, there was a new circumcision and a new food, and now there was a new messenger with a new message. God wanted to cause His people to understand, before they ever set foot on the first battlefield, that He was God. The very next verse of Joshua (6:1) begins, *"Now Jericho."* All of this preliminary activity had been to get God's people to Jericho, where they could begin to possess.

At this point, God sent a special messenger to bring this very important message. The message was this: these people, who loved Him enough to keep their eyes on Him, follow Him and honor Him were so important to Him that they need not worry before each battle how things might go. He was to be Lord of every battle, and their victory would be assured.

As we previously noted, what the older generation knew as warfare was very different from the type of warfare God wanted this new generation to employ. There was a whole new way of doing things, a much higher way. The former generation had done it one way, but the Lord of Hosts would do it in a very different way. He would show up on their behalf, and the battle would be won.

Something New for Their Feet

Then something else new happened. The children of Israel had followed the Ark because God's presence was with it, and they dared not forsake it. Now God was about to take them to a higher level. Every single place where their feet trod would become a holy place. Wherever they placed their foot, the presence of God would be found. Anywhere they went, the presence of God would be there with them. That's why He commanded Joshua to take off his shoe. He would not ever walk in the same way again. As part of a new generation, even his walk would be holy.

> *There was a whole new way of doing things, a much higher way!*

Why This Message Burns So Intensely in My Soul

This message has been burning so intensely in my heart that I've found it difficult to sleep at times.

I'm so grateful for what God is telling us. We often struggle in our Christian walk, but I'm certain that much of our struggle is absolutely needless. Let me tell you how I came to that conclusion.

This message came to me in its present form shortly after my husband and I returned from a ministry trip to South Africa. One of our first nights home, I was feeling God's presence very powerfully. I was in my own bed with my own pillow for a change, and yet sleep seemed far from me. I knew that something was up.

I went into the bathroom, drew some hot water in the tub and got in to soak. Then, suddenly I saw a huge angel reflected in the bathroom mirror. It's a very lovely bathroom with high ceilings, and yet I could only see about half of him. He was that big.

He was clad in armor, and it seemed to be all white, and yet it was all gold. He had a chord trim about him, and it was also gold—and yet it was white.

I sat speechless and in awe and wonderment, afraid that if I turned to see him directly, he would be gone. So I dared not take my eyes off of him.

He moved ever so slightly, and I knew suddenly that he was in charge of our household. One of our air-conditioning units was out of service, and we were living in just two rooms of the house. Our son

Brinsley had been living like that for the two weeks we were away. When the realization came to me that this powerful angel had been sent to protect our house, something leaped inside of me, and I realized that He was none other than the Lord of Hosts Himself.

Actually I wasn't able to put it all together until early the next morning. When I did, I had the sudden urge to tell someone.

But it was 4:30 in the morning. Who would be awake at that hour? I hated to wake my husband, but I felt I had no choice. "Honey," I said, "you've got to wake up. I saw an angel, and I just have to tell somebody." And I began to tell him what the Lord was showing me.

It's a New Day

The Lord was helping me to understand what He had brought us out of and what He had brought us into. My conclusion was that our experiences with spiritual warfare would be very different in the future. Our God says that He is the Lord of the Battle, and when we are struggling with something, that is not His perfect will. His desire is that we be at peace and at rest at all times.

It is true that God tells us in Ephesians 6:

*Therefore put on God's complete armor, that you
may be able to resist and stand your ground on the
evil day [of danger], and having done all [the crisis
demands], to stand [firmly in your place].*

Ephesians 6:13

> *Our
> job
> is
> to
> cut
> off
> anything
> and
> everything
> that
> is
> in
> opposition
> to
> His
> presence!*

But when God says this, He's not telling us that we must fight our own battles. These elements of armor are part of His protection upon us, as we stand watching Him fight in our place.

This is important. God doesn't line us up, give us one last pep talk, and then send us into battle with the cry "Charge!" He doesn't stand back waiting to see how many casualties of war there will be among us. He's the Lord of Hosts, and so our victory is already accomplished.

Our job is to keep our eyes on Him, to follow Him and to honor Him. Our job is to cut off anything and everything that is in opposition to His presence. Then, we're not to struggle with every evil that comes our way. God will do that on our behalf.

If each of us could come to understand our covenant with God, we would have much less sickness and disease. That's what circumcision was all about. It was a cutting away of anything that would prevent a person from receiving everything God had for them. It was not a punishment; it was a door to promise.

Jesus Shed His Blood Once and for All

Jesus shed His blood for us, once and for all, and He says to each of us today, "If you're still struggling, know that you don't need to. Stop struggling and accept the fullness of My finished redemption."

All of us have been blessed in life, but what we have received to date is nothing compared with what God still has waiting for us. As we can learn not to struggle for everything, but to receive what He has already done for us, we can multiply the blessings over our life. The more you let God take care of the battles, the healthier you will be. Stop struggling and focus on Him, and let Him take care of everything for you.

We miss many blessings because we insist on fighting our own battles. Let the Lord of Hosts care for you. Then you can cross over and possess the land.

Joshua "Looked Up"

Joshua *"looked up."* How interesting!

Isaiah had a similar experience. When King Uzziah died, he *"saw the Lord ... high and lifted up"* (Isaiah 6:1). The original language used here suggests that Joshua was looking with a prophetic eye or with prophetic insight. He was not simply staring into space, wondering, "Okay, God, what's next?" He had begun to understand that he was inheriting something great, and he was waiting on God for guidance to know just how to proceed with it. It was with this anticipation that Joshua *"looked up."* It was an expectant looking.

It's not until the old has been cut off and you have entered into covenant with God that you can begin to look into the future and see what it is that He will do. Only then can you fully understand. Only then can you come into the revelation of it. You can't do it with "stuff" stuck to you. You can't do it while you're eating the old manna. You must rise to revelation.

Looking up will give you strength to rise above your circumstances. It will cause you to peer into the wisdom and greatness and revelation of what God is saying, and in the process, you will begin to see into the prophetic realm.

The Man Was In Front of Him

When Joshua looked up, he began to see something beyond the natural. A man stood there *"over against him," "opposite him," "facing him,"* or *"in front of him"*—depending on the translation you happen to be reading. *"In front of him"* may be the best translation. Whatever the case, when Joshua began to look up prophetically, he suddenly saw, by the Spirit, what was just ahead of him.

The *"Man"* (capitalized in several translations) had a drawn sword in His hand. Joshua approached Him and asked the question: *"Are you for us or for our adversaries?"* The answer was interesting:

> *And He said, No [neither], but as Prince of the Lord's host have I now come.*   Joshua 5:14

With that, Joshua *"fell on his face"*:

> *And Joshua fell on his face to the earth and worshiped, and said to Him, What says my Lord to His servant?*   Joshua 5:14

Every time we go into battle, we need an encounter with the Lord of Battle, and the intensity of our encounter with Him will determine the outcome of our battles. Where we put our focus, therefore, is all-important. Joshua could have fixed his gaze on Jericho, that first prize city, and concentrated his encounter on that goal. Instead, he looked up and saw the Lord.

It would not have been unusual for Joshua, at that particular moment, to be examining with intensity the fortifications of Jericho and its defenders. Instead, he chose to look up, to look higher than the problem, higher than the challenge at hand. Thus, in his looking, he began to experience something deeper.

The Man Had a Drawn Sword

The *Man* not only had a sword in His hand; that sword was *drawn*. It was therefore evident to Joshua that this *Man* had come to do battle, and the only question pending was which side he would fight on. So, Joshua asked the question. The *Man* was obviously big and strong and powerful, and Joshua wanted to know where He stood.

Are you with us? Or are you with them? Which side will you fight on? The answer was one that would have confused me. The *Man* said He was not on either side; He had come to represent the Lord in this battle.

I would not have liked that answer. I would have wanted a *Man* such as this to be on my team, and the fact that He chose to remain neutral would have seemed troubling to me.

This Was God Himself

When Moses encountered the burning bush (see Exodus 2), he heard God's voice, but he didn't actually see God. Now God chose to appear to Joshua. This was no angel or heavenly messenger; this was God Himself. He had not come to choose sides in this battle. He had come because He was Captain, or Prince, of the Lord's Hosts.

What did this mean? In reality, the battle was already rigged in Joshua's favor. The Captain of the Lord's Hosts would fight and win. In other words, God was telling Joshua, "Because of everything you've done (you've made covenant with Me, you've circumcised the new generation, you've eaten fresh grain, and you've set yourself aside to look up to Me), I want you to know that I will not appear to you simply as a voice, as I did with Moses at the burning bush. I will appear to you in physical form so that you will know that I am Captain of the Host.

> *I want to tell you that the battle is already won!*

"The older generation taught themselves to war. In their own sufficiency, their own knowledge and their own strength, they accomplished it. You will do things in a new way. I want to tell you that the battle is already won. You can go up and take the city. I have given it to you. Before any trumpet is blown to call men to battle, and before you march forth to face the first enemy soldier, I have given you victory. It is an accomplished fact."

The Lord of Hosts was not appearing to tell Joshua what strategy to use in the upcoming battle. He was appearing to tell him that he would not even have to fight. The battle was won. That's what covenant with God is all about.

God keeps covenant with us, and part of His covenant is that He will appear as Lord of Hosts whenever we need His help. The salvation of your loved ones is already accomplished. Every battle has been rigged in your favor. You are victorious through our God. Begin to possess what is already yours because of your position in Christ.

Joshua Cast Himself Down

When the *Man* said, *"As Prince of the Lord's hosts have I now come,"* that's when Joshua fell on his face. In the original, the wording meant "to cast oneself down." Joshua actually cast himself down before the Lord, and this says a lot about Joshua. Despite the fact that he had a covenant with God, that he now knew much more about God and His workings, and that he was now positioned in a special way for blessing from God, when he knew he was in the presence of the living God, he fell on his face in reverence and awe.

Joshua knew that God's presence merits our respect. He had been having some powerful experiences, but when he knew he was in God's presence, he very deliberately cast himself face down before the Lord and worshiped. That act speaks volumes.

It's so sad to me that we have to practically beg people to worship God these days. It's sad that we now require special music and special sound systems before people are willing to worship God. He is a loving God who keeps covenant, despite all the stinking things we do, and He is therefore worthy of all our praise. How sad that we have to keep coming up with new programs to keep people's interest and keep them coming to the House of God!

God sees us, He cares for us, and He provides for us, and yet we have to practically stand on our heads to get people to worship Him. That's sad!

Joshua's First Duty

Joshua understood that his first duty was to respect and worship God, and even though he was a mighty man of power and authority, he didn't hesitate a moment to humble himself before God and worship Him. That's the mark of a great man.

Yes, God keeps covenant with us, but what seals our relationship with Him is our worship. He doesn't ask much of us, only that we love Him and that we let Him know that we love Him. And the way we do that is through our worship.

Each of us has favorite songs of worship and favorite sounds and rhythms. But is it ever right to stand back in times of public worship with our arms folded and refuse to participate because we don't like the sound or the rhythm of the music being used? I think not!

> *The problem with my will is that it likes itself too much!*

"Oh, I love those old hymns," some of the older saints among us say. "I wish they would sing those more." You can't please everyone. Some, if you don't sing what they want to sing, refuse to worship.

Even a good "Hallelujah" would be wonderful!

Try a big "Holy"! That should do it.

Try this one: "Worthy"! That should do it.

Try something. Don't just stand there. The God of the Universe is waiting for you to open your mouth and offer Him some type of praise.

The mere knowledge that he was in the presence of God was cause enough for Joshua. He immediately cast himself down and worshiped. He didn't need any coaxing or coaching. He was ready to wor-ship God at a moment's notice.

The Second Amazing Thing

Then Joshua did the second amazing thing. He asked, *"What says my Lord to His servant?"* Today God is working in us as never before to convince us to be willing to bend our will to His. This seems to be the most difficult step any of us could be asked to take.

We all grow up basically self-willed, and it seems like the most difficult thing in the world to be will-ing to change. This is what got the children of Israel in trouble over and over again, and it's what many Christians are struggling with even now.

The Bible has much to say about strong-willed people, and I'm sad to say that there are many of them in the Body of Christ. They run around acting like they're important. They are unbridled and refuse to be submitted to anyone. They insist on doing their own little thing, and they want everyone to think they're important as they're doing it. Some churches are full of them.

Such people refuse to bend to the Father's will, let alone the will of those in church leadership. They're not about to bend to anyone. If you agree with what they want, they're fine for a while, but the minute you no longer agree, they're off to their own little corner of the universe, where they can control things.

These people are always on the move. They're moving from one church to another, from one marriage to another, from one job to another, and from one bank to another. The minute they find someone who's not in total agreement with them, they're gone. But what did Jesus say when He prayed:

Not My will, but [always] Yours be done.

Luke 22:42

He said, "Always!" And He was God in the flesh.

The Problem with My Will

The problem with my will is that it likes itself too much. Given the choice, it will always choose itself over the will of others—even the will of God. I must surrender my will to God and accept His will for my life. That's exactly what Paul meant when he wrote:

I die daily.   1 Corinthians 15:31

Paul died to self, so that he could live unto God.

Because God is God, He always knows what's best for us. That's why doing His will is the very best decision we could possibly make. Paul relinquished his own desires every day for the higher purposes of God. His own will had to bend, and he had to let God have His way.

What does it mean to crucify your flesh? If your flesh dies, you'll be gone from this world, won't you? What God is requiring of us is a spiritual death, a death of self. The reason is this: In order for you to accomplish what you are called to accomplish in the Kingdom of God, your will must be surrendered to God's will. This is part of your circumcision, part of the cutting off of the things that hinder you. God wants your spirit to remain active, but He wants your will to surrender. As long as you remain seated on the throne of your will, God can never do through you what He has called you to do in life. He must own your will. That's all there is to it.

The Israelites were so self-willed that they would rather go back into bondage in Egypt than not have their own way. That's why they got left behind in the wilderness, and those who wanted to enter the land had to circumcise themselves, cutting off the self-will.

Can you imagine those men and women being willing to return to that hated life of slavery and misery rather than surrender their will to God and to His man? That's how strong the will of man is. God was ready to give these men and women something their forefathers had never possessed, but their will prevented them from receiving it. WOW!

Your Will Controls Everything Around You

Your will controls your worship. It controls your reaction or lack of reaction to God's Spirit. It controls your relationship with your fellowman. Your will often keeps you from forgiving those who have wronged you. It would rather live in bitterness than let go of the hurts and offenses of the past. It makes you seek revenge, when you know that's not the right and healthy thing to do.

In the world around us today, the strong will of men and women (and boys and girls) is considered to be nothing more than a little behavioral problem. "Let's try them on this new medication and see if it corrects the behavior," some suggest. "We have a wide variety of drugs available to us, and they have very few side effects." What they don't seem to understand is that the real problem is simply that the person involved refuses to bend his or her will. They're stubborn. That's all. And they'll have to learn the hard way.

What should we do with children who are will-
ful? The Bible says that we should spank them. If
not, we will be put *"to shame":*

*The rod and reproof give wisdom,
but a child left undisciplined
brings his mother to shame.
Correct your son, and he will
give you rest; yes, he will give
delight to your heart.*
Proverbs 29:15 and 17

God Chastens those Whom He Loves

What can God do with you
when your will refuses to bend?
He has no alternative but to chas-
ten you:

*Know also in your [minds and]
hearts that, as a man disciplines
and instructs his son, so the
Lord your God disciplines and
instructs you.*
Deuteronomy 8:5

*[Your
will]
would
rather
live
in
bitterness
than
let
go
of
the
hurts
and
offenses
of
the
past!*

*For the Lord corrects and disciplines everyone
whom He loves, and He punishes, even scourges,*

every son whom He accepts and welcomes to His heart and cherishes. You must submit to and endure [correction] for discipline: God is dealing with you as with sons. For what son is there whom his father does not [thus] train and correct and discipline.

Now if you are exempt from correction and left without discipline in which all [of God's children] share, then you are illegitimate offspring and not true sons [at all]. Hebrews 12:6-8

If we can learn to accept the chastening of the Lord, it will do wonders for us.

Worship Leads to Yielding

It was in worship that Joshua was able to bend His will and ask God what He wanted of him. He couldn't worship on his face before God and then get up and act like nothing had happened or get up and act like he had before. Worship changes everything. To worship God on his face and then get up and live like he wanted to would have been two-faced, and Joshua couldn't do that.

If you are intent on doing your own thing, then forget about worshiping God. The two don't go together. Worship demands submission. If God is worthy of our worship, He is also worthy of our obedience. If He is God, then He knows best, and we should willingly and joyfully follow His will. If you are unwilling to yield to Him, then it would be better not to even worship Him in the first place, because your worship is nothing more than a sham.

The new generation of the children of Israel had a new opportunity, they experienced a new circumcision, they ate a new food, and they met a new messenger. What would come next?

CHAPTER 5

The New Experience

Then the Commander of the LORD's army said to Joshua, "Take your sandal off your foot, for the place where you stand is holy." And Joshua did so.
Joshua 5:15, NKJ

Take Off One Shoe

"What do you want me to do, Lord?" is the question that logically follows true worship. When Joshua asked this question, something very interesting happened. The Lord told him to take off one of his shoes.

> "What do you want me to do, Lord?" is the question that logically follows true worship!

The original language, in this case, spoke of just one *"shoe,"* or *"sandal,"* and just one *"foot,"* not *"feet,"* as the Amplified Bible renders it. In Moses' case, it had been *"shoes,"* or *"sandals"* and *"feet,"* but not here. Here it was only one.

When Moses had his encounter at the burning bush, God told him to take off his shoes, for it was holy ground. This signified that his will was now to be bent to the Father's will, and God would direct his footsteps in the future. And where did his footsteps take him? Around and around in circles in the wilderness for forty years. Now something very different was happening to Joshua.

There is one similarity in the two cases. The ground where Joshua was standing was also declared to be holy ground. There the similarities end, for Joshua was asked to remove just one shoe from just one foot.

Why Just One Shoe?

Why would God want just one shoe removed from just one foot? The answer is that in olden days, when people entered into a covenant with each other, and one of them was considered to be the lesser of the two (meaning that he didn't have as much to offer, or share, as the other party), he would remove one of his shoes and give it to his covenant partner as a sign of their agreement. This signified the recognition that the greater partner would have no difficulty keeping his part of the bargain. He had the means to fulfill all. The lesser of the parties, the weaker of the two, would have more difficulty fulfilling his part of the bargain.

By removing one shoe, the other partner in the agreement was saying, "I may be the weaker partner in this covenant, and I may have less to give, but I will keep my covenants." Therefore, when God asked Joshua for only one shoe, He was reminding him which of them was God and which of them was man, which of them had all power and which of them was limited. From that day forward, whenever Joshua was about to go into battle, he could know that he didn't have to win the victory in his own strength. He was incapable of doing so, but he was assured that God would do it for him.

God Was the Stronger Partner

God knew all about Jericho; Joshua knew only the obvious and visible things about that famous city. In every way, Joshua was the weaker of the two, so now he was required to surrender to the Greater, He who had already won the battle.

Why not take your shoe off today and hold it up to God in recognition of His greatness and your surrender to that greatness? Don't be ashamed or afraid to do this. You have nothing to lose. The places God has prepared for you and the things He has prepared for you in those places will not come to you because of your own strength. Let Him be God, and He can open every door to you, remove every obstacle and give you victory over every enemy.

You are not God, but if you know God, that's enough. He desires to enter into a binding covenant with you to do for you what you cannot do for yourself. As a token of your willingness to walk with Him, lift up one shoe to Him today.

God Commits Himself to You

The God of the Universe now offers to commit

Himself and His resources to you—if you're willing to commit your all to Him. What a bargain! What a deal! How could you refuse such an offer?

What you cannot do on your own, you can do through the strength of the God of your covenant. He will never break covenant with you. Can you say the same today?

God will do what He said He will do. He will perform His Word. He will fulfill His every promise. Will you do your part?

It doesn't matter today how hopeless your case might seem, it doesn't matter how many times you may have been denied in the past, and it doesn't matter how farfetched your promises from God may appear to others. If God said it, He will do it. You can count on Him. God will keep His word; will you keep yours?

What Will Your Choice Be?

Will you choose to worship Him? Will you choose to serve Him? Will you choose to be faithful to Him? Will you refuse to crumble in the face of opposition? Will you remember His greatness in your life? God keeps His covenant promises; will you keep yours?

When you're in the heat of battle and are facing imminent danger, that's not the time to begin to examine to see if your covenant with God is in order.

You have to know it going into the battle. Don't wait until you're facing the formidable defenses of Jericho before you decide to go back and make things right with God. Have your mind made up going in. Position yourself ahead of time. Make sure you keep your part of the covenant. You can always count on God to keep His.

Make Sure You're Not the Weak Link

Remind yourself often of God's faithfulness and His goodness. Then make sure that you're not the weak link in this agreement. Do your part.

Only two people know what's in your heart—you and God. Only you and God can know if your will is totally submitted to His. No one else can give you a spiritual checkup and determine if you're doing the right thing. Examine yourself today, and make sure you're keeping your end of the deal.

Don't ever doubt God, and don't ever run from Him. Run toward God, fling yourself into His loving arms and say, "Lord, You're the Greater One. You have no problem keeping Your covenant. As for me, I'm not deity, but deity lives inside of me. With Your help, I will fulfill my part of the agreement. With Your help, I will be faithful.

"I will believe You, trust You, depend on You, and rely on You. I will not falter or fail. I will not quit. I will not become discouraged. I will not turn back. I will go forward.

"I will worship. I will bow down. I will give honor to You. I will bend my will to Your will. I will surrender to Your purpose in my life."

God Was Asking for His Promise

By asking Joshua for his shoe, God was asking for his word, his promise, his covenant. The shoe was a token of Joshua's agreement to keep his end of the bargain, and that was enough for God.

Hold that shoe up to God today and walk around a little with it held high. Show Him that you mean business, that you're serious about this agreement, that you sense the severity of the covenant you have with Him today.

A new generation of the children of Israel had a new opportunity, they experienced a new circumcision, they ate a new food, they were visited by a new messenger with a new message, and they had a new experience.

It was time to cross over and begin to possess all that God had reserved for them.

> *If God said it, He will do it. You can count on Him!*

Part II

Crossing Over and Possessing

CHAPTER 6

Crossing Your Jordans

So ... the people set out from their tents to pass over the Jordan, with the priests bearing the ark of the covenant before. Joshua 3:14

Crossing Day

As we have seen, the people were given specific instructions about how they were to proceed. The most important of these instructions was that the presence of the Lord was always to go before them. If the Lord of Hosts went before them, He would take care of everything, preparing the way for them to follow. So the priests led the way, bearing the Ark:

> *And when those who bore the ark had come to the Jordan and the feet of the priests bearing the ark were in the brink of the water—for the Jordan overflows all its banks throughout the time of harvest—then the waters that came down from above stood and rose up in a heap far off, at Adam, the city that is beside Zarethan; and those flowing down toward the Sea of Arabah, the Salt [Dead] Sea, were wholly cut off. And the people passed over opposite Jericho.* Joshua 3:15-16

It was the time of harvest, and the Jordan was at flood stage. It was overflowing its banks, and was, consequently, a much larger river than it was the rest of the year. As a result, the Israelites needed a larger-than-normal miracle at that moment. And they got it. The waters of the Jordan, as far as the city of Adam, were pushed up in a heap, so that they could safely cross over.

Twenty Miles of Dry Riverbed

The city of Adam was situated some sixteen miles upstream from Jericho, so it seems that a stretch of some twenty to thirty miles of riverbed were left dry as the people passed over. It is estimated that the river may have been one to two miles wide at that place. Can you imagine two or three million people passing over the Jordan? What a sight that must have been!

Even though the river was at flood stage, God picked up the water and moved it back some twenty miles so that His people could cross. That was not at all "normal"; it was extraordinary.

> *That was not at all "normal"; it was extraordinary!*

God had done a similar thing at the Red Sea, but the people had not fully appreciated it. Yes, they did a little thanksgiving dance after they got to the other side, but after that, the matter was pretty much removed from their minds. As they went about their daily tasks, they were not remembering the God who divides the seas and rolls back rivers so that His people can cross. It wasn't long after their token time of praise that they were back to their usual grumbling and griping.

But this was a new generation, and whatever comes our way, we must declare: *"I can do all things through Christ"* (Philippians 4:13, KJV). The Amplified Bible says it this way:

> *I have strength for all things in Christ Who empowers me [I am ready for anything through Him Who infuses inner strength into me; I am self-sufficient in Christ's sufficiency].*

This is all due to the fact that we have covenant with God. We are the head and not the tail because we have covenant with Him. We won't go under because we have covenant with Him. We will go through because we have covenant with the Lord of Hosts. None of it is to our own credit.

We're a new breed, a new generation, and we'll be victorious, not because we have somehow become perfect (we still have a long way to go on that point), but because we're in covenant with God. That guarantees us victory every time.

Some people confess victory, but they can't live it because they don't have covenant with God. Confessing victory is important, but it's never enough.

How Did It Happen?

When those waters stood and rose up in a heap, Moses was not there with his rod stretched out. In fact, no mention is made of a rod being used at all. As the body of people moved forward that day, no one particular man or woman was found out front leading the rest.

Yes, the priests were there at the vanguard, but this was a corporate movement. All the priests put their foot in the water at the same time. When the victory was won, they would not be able to give the glory to any one man. They had all stepped in together, and they all went over together.

The leadership style of Joshua was to be very different from that of Moses. There was no hoopla with Joshua. He simply announced what they would all do the following day, and then they all set about to do it. That's all there was to it.

And that's how the Lord wants it to be with us today. His desire is that we hear His voice, and then just get up and do it. We shouldn't have to wait for some spectacular announcement on the nightly television news. If God is speaking, we should be obeying.

God Was Doing His Part

When the people did their part, God did His part. Suddenly, no water was flowing into the Dead Sea.

God had cut the waters off upstream. The riverbed became dry and stayed dry as all the people passed over:

> *And while all Israel passed over on dry ground, the priests who bore the ark of the covenant of the Lord stood firm on dry ground in the midst of the Jordan, until all the nation finished passing over the Jordan.*
>
> Joshua 3:17

> *Our covenant demands that certain monuments be erected to cause us to remember the goodness of God!*

They all passed over. Praise God! And you can pass over your Jordan too. What are you waiting for? Get started today.

Marking the Place

It's interesting to note what the Lord told the people next. They were to pick up stones and mark their crossing so that it would never be forgotten:

When all the nation had passed over the Jordan, the Lord said to Joshua, Take twelve men from among the people, one man out of every tribe, and command them, Take twelve stones out of the midst of the Jordan from the place where the priests' feet stood firm; carry them over with you and leave them at the place where you lodge tonight.   Joshua 4:1-3

Our covenant demands that certain monuments be erected to cause us to remember the goodness of God to us at certain points. How could the people have kept forgetting the crossing of the Red Sea? Apparently they had not set up enough monuments to remind themselves of it. This must not happen again, so they erected some monuments to assure that it didn't.

The older generation had not only forgotten the crossing of the Red Sea; they forgot that water came out of a rock to give them a drink when they desperately needed it. They forgot that quail had come down from Heaven when they needed meat. God's provisions for them had been daily and supernatural, and yet they had found room for complaints. Why? Could it be that they didn't really know God? What a tragic thought!

It's doubly tragic to see how very little some church people seem to know God today. A new generation must make sure that it has a monument and that it never forgets the goodness of God. We must know that He is God and that He keeps covenant with His people.

A Monument in the Midst of the River

Aside from the twelve stones carried by twelve men out of the midst of the Jordan, Joshua set up another monument made of twelve stones. It was erected on the very spot where the feet of the priests had rested while all the people crossed safely over to the other side.

Once the water from the Jordan had returned to its place, no one would be able to see these particular stones. Only God could then see them. So what did they mean? It had taken a step of faith to move into the waters of the Jordan, and God saw that step of faith and marked it. Again today, He is looking for those who will believe Him — in spite of their Jordans. And when you take a step of faith, He will mark it.

Believe God in spite of all circumstances! Trust Him anyway! How you feel about the situation at the moment is beside the point. You must cross through the waters of your Jordan.

There will surely be some Jordans in your life, and God is looking for a people who will extend their faith and then step forward — stepping, stepping, stepping by faith.

The people would never see these particular stones again, but God never forgot them. They were there as a monument to the faith of His people. They had kept covenant with Him.

They Needed to Remember

The twelve stones that were carried out of Jordan built a monument the people could see and remember. God said it was for their children and for all succeeding generations, but it was for this new generation too. They needed to remember, as they faced their next Jordan in life.

What was it they needed to remember? How great they were? No. They needed to remember that God keeps covenant. He keeps His word. He honors His promises. If you will do your part, God will always do His.

Covenant Is Personal

Entering into a covenant with God is a very personal thing. It cannot be formed between three people, not this kind of covenant, anyway. I'm crazy about my husband after thirty-nine years of marriage, and I love him more today than I've ever loved him before, but still my covenant with God is personal, and ranks higher than my relationship with my husband.

Where my relationship with God is concerned, my husband can't step in. He can't make it better, and he can't make it worse. He can't fix anything that's not right, and there's nothing that he can change about it. It's all between me and God.

That's why there's no open heaven over you if you have no covenant with God. You have no right to His blessings, and you cannot lay claim to His promises of safety. Without a relationship with God, you have nothing.

Build Your Own Monuments

I want to encourage you to build monuments in your life that will remind you and yours of the goodness of the Lord. Please don't forget what He's done for you. When I preached this message in our church, I asked the Lord how we could apply it in a practical way. He showed me to have one of our men collect some stones from our driveway. Then, at the close of the sermon, we handed these stones out to the people and allowed them to use them to build a monument to the goodness of God in their lives.

I had thought of taking communion that morning, and we could have done it, but God said we needed to go deeper. We were believers, and we could easily have partaken of His body and blood, but we needed to be reminded that He loved us when we were unlovely. He gave Himself for us when we didn't deserve it. He still loves us, even when we're too angry with Him to respond.

As we took those stones and began to think of the goodness of God, I encouraged everyone present not to think of God in terms of things. This was not a time to be asking Him to meet our electric bill. He already knew about that. If we remembered Him and His goodness, He would do the rest. Forgetting the goodness of God brings on worry, but remembering His goodness removes every care.

> *Forgetting the goodness of God brings on worry, but remembering His goodness removes every care!*

It's Worth Remembering

As we stood before the Lord that day, I remembered a day twenty-five years before when I'd had no washer and dryer and two babies to care for. When looking for an apartment, we had taken the step of faith of choosing an apartment that had a hookup for washer and dryer (not all of them did). Then one day someone came to visit, and before leaving, they wrote out a check to us for enough to purchase a washer and dryer. I can never forget that day. Those machines lasted us for the next twenty-five years.

An experience like that is worth remembering. It's worth building a monument to. If you can't remember the goodness of God in your past, how can you trust Him with your future?

I still remember miracles God did for my parents, so I can't get down about today or tomorrow. God is faithful. He always has been, and He always will be.

May God forgive us for taking Him for granted, for being cold and indifferent to Him, for putting our trust in other things and not in Him. Let us remember today so that we can continue to cross over and conquer the land.

Just that Easily

Just that easily, the Jordan, that long-feared barrier, was passed over, and the Israelites found themselves on the other side. What excitement must have filled their hearts at that moment. One giant step had been taken, and soon they would take others.

Soon they would begin to possess the land, town by town, and plot by plot. For now, they must prepare. They had crossed this Jordan, but there were other Jordans yet to cross. There were giants to fight and cities to conquer. But at last, victory was within sight. They slept that night within visible sight of Jericho, the first prize.

CHAPTER 7

Crossing Over the Walls Of Your Jerichos

So the people shouted, and the trumpets were blown. When the people heard the sound of the trumpet, they raised a great shout, and [Jericho's] wall fell down in its place, so that the [Israelites] went up into the city, every man straight before him, and they took the city.   Joshua 6:20

Their Presence Generated Fear

Before we proceed to the taking of Jericho, we must note what the mere presence of the Israelites had already accomplished. As Chapter 5 of Joshua opens, we find the kings beyond Jordan disturbed by what they saw happening:

> We should have such power with God that the news of it causes the hearts of our enemies to melt!

When all the kings of the Amorites who were beyond the Jordan to the west and all the kings of the Canaanites who were by the sea heard that the Lord had dried up the waters of the Jordan before the Israelites until we had crossed over, their hearts melted and there was no spirit in them any more because of the Israelites. Joshua 5:1-2

This is exactly what will happen to your enemy when you fear God, keep your eyes on Him, follow Him and honor Him in all things. These kings were not afraid of a group of ragtag former slaves from Egypt, but they *were* afraid of their God and of His power. The older generation of Israelites had feared the inhabitants of the land, and this fear had caused them to miss their inheritance. Now, the inhabitants of the land feared the children of God. That's the way it should be.

As the people prepared themselves to go into the land, God caused fear in the hearts of their enemies, and I believe with all my heart that this is what the Lord wants to do for the Church today. Our hearts are never to melt at the news of the enemy's activities. We should have such power with God that the news of it causes the hearts of our enemies to melt.

It's time for us to rise up to the place that simply our speaking the name of Jesus causes the heart of the enemy to melt. As we rise in corporate prayer and we rise and come together to act in the name of God, it should cause enemies to flee on every side.

There must be a reversal. We can no longer run in fear of Satan. He must now run in fear of us. What is happening in the Kingdom of God and what is happening in our everyday lives must be, for every enemy, a cause for alarm.

It didn't take many miracles at the hand of God to bring about this fear in the hearts of the Amorites and Canaanites. They just heard about the opening of the River Jordan, and that was enough. Just one miracle caused them to be afraid.

It All Happened within Sight of Jericho

It is good to remind ourselves again that many of the new things the Israelites were experiencing came within sight of Jericho. From their camp, they could clearly see the first enemy city they would face.

As we saw, the men had been circumcised right there, making them vulnerable to attack. God had required that it be done in this way so that He could show them His superiority to any enemy. He is God over your Jerichos, too, and He will make you sit for a time in enemy territory to prove to you that He is God over your enemies as well.

"Why do I have to sit here and take this?" you may sometimes wonder. God's proving a point to you. He can cause you to camp in enemy territory, and you'll survive it. This fight is rigged in your favor, so relax.

Have you ever watched professional wrestling? It's worse than a soap opera. It's all play acting. Every fight is choreographed in advance.

Well, Satan doesn't seem to know it yet, but all of his posturing and all of his bravado is for naught. God has your victory signed, sealed and delivered, and whatever comical moves Satan makes will not change that fact. You just need to understand why you're sitting in the place you are, waiting for your answer, waiting for the defeat of your enemy, waiting for justice in your case. It's coming.

In the meantime, will you complain? Will you decide to return to the old? If you want to return to that round-and-round rat race, that's your decision. God's will is for you to move forward and cross over into your inheritance.

Jericho Was "Shut Up"

Now Jericho [a fenced town with high walls] was tightly closed because of the Israelites; no one went out or came in.   Joshua 6:1

The King James Version of the Bible says it this way:

Now Jericho was straitly shut up because of the children of Israel: none went out, and none came in.

I hear the Lord saying something to Jericho, that enemy city. "Jericho, shut up." And Jericho had to shut up, or shut itself up.

Jericho was tightly shut because its people feared the Israelites, and, as we noted, this is where the Church should be today. Because of the hand of God upon our lives, the people of the world around us should have a fearful respect.

I'm convinced that the men of Jericho had been working feverishly to improve their already-strong walls. Now that the Israelites were getting closer, they ordered their city to be completely closed and sealed. No one was allowed in, and no one was allowed out.

We're always expecting our victories to come easily, and we seem to be surprised when the enemy hits us twice as hard as we expect. We do a little Jericho march on Sunday, and when we wake up on Monday, we expect everything to go well. Instead, all hell seems to break loose around us. Get used to it. Satan knows what's coming, and he gets ready for it.

Because the people of the Jericho area were in awe over what the children of Israel had accomplished, they quickly fortified themselves, determining to show God's people what a stronghold was really like. Jericho had been a protected place with a high wall around it. Now, it was doubly protected. Of course, that didn't hinder God:

"See!"

And the Lord said to Joshua, See, I have given Jericho, its king, and mighty men of valor, into your hands. Joshua 6:2

"See!" What could Joshua *see*? To him, the city looked more formidable than ever, but God wanted him to see the situation in the Spirit. *"See,"* He said, *"I have given you the city."* This is an important point. We need to see as God sees because what you see is what you get.

These two phrases, *"See"* and *"I have given you the city"* go together. We look at the second phrase, *"I have given you the city,"* and we wonder why God's not doing it. But the truth is that we're focusing on every negative aspect of our situation, and we haven't yet seen things from God's perspective. You have to see something in the Spirit before you can have it.

When God told Joshua, *"See,"* it was imperative. It was a command. You must see. You can't get what God is promising you without first letting Him open the eyes of your understanding to see it.

> *You have to see something in the Spirit before you can have it!*

See it, and you will have it. See it, and it will be yours. Fail to see it, and all bets are off.

The receiving never comes first. It's always the seeing that has to come first. This is a spiritual principle, a Kingdom principle. If Joshua could *see* victory, then he could *have* victory.

In the natural, the walls around Jericho were impregnable. They were fully twenty feet thick, we are told. That didn't look very good. So Joshua could not look at those walls and expect to have victory.

Some have imagined that God was saying, "See that wall. I've given it to you." But that's not what He was saying. Joshua had to see himself taking the city. He had to see the city in his possession. If he focused on the wall itself, he would have been discouraged.

The root word, translated here as *"see,"* means "to advise yourself, to make ready to enjoy an experience." It means "let your vision be joyful." That's what Joshua had to do to inherit Jericho. What you see you can inherit.

What did the Lord mean when He said, *"I have given Jericho ... into your hands."* He meant "I have assigned, I have appointed, I have fastened, I have framed, I have recompensed, I have restored, I have given back your power, your credit, your dominion, your charge ... with extra." That sounds like victory to me.

Jericho Had to Come First

The children of Israel could not enter the land of Canaan without first conquering Jericho. It was the first city on their list because it protected the border of the land. If they had looked upon it in the natural, they would have been disappointed, and the older generation, made up of murmurers and rebels, surely would have made this mistake. This new generation could not afford to do so.

This new generation had a new covenant, and they had the Lord of Hosts with them, so they had a whole different outlook. And this is exactly what the Lord wants to do for you and for me this very day. He wants to give us spiritual eyes. How you think about a particular circumstance and how you react to it are important. If you think and react in the old way, you'll miss it. It's all related to how you see God and His power in your life.

The City, Its King and Its Mighty Men

God said, *"See, I have given Jericho, its king, and mighty men of valor, into your hands."* Of everything in this particular chapter of Joshua, here's the thing that always amazes me the most. This verse lays out a strategy for a successful battle: Jericho, its king and its mighty men. Those were the goals of conquest. Jericho was an ancient stronghold, and it could be taken only if its king and its mighty men were somehow defeated.

In warfare, there are important elements. Paul wrote to the early Church:

For we are not wrestling with flesh and blood [contending only with physical opponents], but against the despotisms, against the powers, against [the master spirits who are] the world rulers of this present darkness, in the heavenly (supernatural) sphere.　　　　Ephesians 6:12

The King James Version says it this way:

For we wrestle not against flesh and blood, but against principalities, against powers, against the rulers of the darkness of this world, against spiritual wickedness in high places.

These represented layers of strongholds. In the past, we have been accustomed to exhausting ourselves wrestling with these various powers, but no more. It's a new day. The Lord of the Battle is with us, and we no longer need to struggle for what is ours.

> *I'm convinced that our strategies must change if we're to conquer all that pertains to us!*

God Must Receive All the Glory

The children of Israel were given specific instructions about how to handle the powers of Jericho. In the process, God would get all the glory, not man. We're not to brag about what we've done, how we've done it or when. It's not about our personal strategy or leadership. He alone is the Lord of the Hosts.

Why does He even need those of us who make up His hosts? He doesn't. He just gives us the privilege of participating. All He needs from us is our obedience. We just need to stand on His side and watch Him do it all. The struggle has been taken out of every battle.

If you're up against your Jerichos, and you have a pick in your hand, trying to take down the wall piece by piece, you're in trouble. And that's just what most of us do.

No one believes in spiritual warfare more than my husband and I do, but I'm convinced that our strategies must change if we're to conquer all that pertains to us. The old ways just won't get it done now fast enough.

The moment we enter the struggle, we bypass the Lord of the Hosts, when He has already fought the battle and won. Our position must be to stand and watch Him do it.

Ready?

Joshua was now to go back and tell the people what must be done:

You shall march around the enclosure, all the men of war going around the city once. This you shall do for six days.   Joshua 6:3

What was spiritual about that? On several occasions, we marched around our church building believing God for victory, and since our building sits right beside Interstate 55, we wondered what people driving by might think of us.

Well, what about Jericho and its people? They were enemies of the Israelites. What must they have been thinking in these moments?

The instructions were for seven days of activity:

And seven priests shall bear forth the ark seven trumpets of rams' horns; and on the seventh day you shall march around the enclosure seven times, and the priests shall blow the trumpets. When they make a long blast with the ram's horn and you hear the sound of the trumpet, all the people shall shout with a great shout; and the wall of the enclosure shall fall down in its place and the people shall go up [over it], every man straight before him.   Joshua 6:4-5

Joshua may not have understood it all, but he obeyed:

So Joshua son of Nun called the priests and said to them, Take up the ark of the covenant and let seven priests bear seven trumpets of rams' horns before the ark of the Lord. He said to the people, Go on! March around the enclosure, and let the armed men pass on before the ark of the Lord.

Joshua 6:6-7

Whether the priests understood it or not, they obeyed:

When Joshua had spoken to the people, the seven priests bearing the seven trumpets of rams' horns passed on before the Lord and blew the trumpets, and the ark of the covenant of the Lord followed them. The armed men went before the priests who blew the trumpets, and the rear guard came after the ark, the priests blowing the trumpets as they went. But Joshua commanded the people, You shall not shout or let your voice be heard, nor shall any word proceed out of your mouth until the day I tell you to shout. Then you shall shout!

Joshua 6:8-10

The first day of this campaign seemed to be fairly uneventful:

*So he caused the ark of the Lord to go around the
city once; and they came into the camp and lodged
in the camp.* Joshua 6:11

The first day had ended — without either obvious
victory or obvious defeat. What would the next days
bring? More of the same:

*Joshua rose early in the morning and the priests
took up the ark of the Lord.* Joshua 6:12

What was going on? Was anything at all
happening?

The Significance of the Number Seven

It's important for us to understand just how
vital it was for the Israelites to carry out their
instructions to the letter. Seven is the number of
completion:

*And the SEVEN priests bearing the SEVEN
trumpets of rams' horns before the ark of the Lord
passed on, blowing the trumpets continually; and
the armed men went before them and the rear guard
came after the ark of the Lord, the priests blowing the
trumpets as they went.* Joshua 6:13

The placement of every individual at Jericho was wonderfully symbolic and important. The most important position in the battle was taken up by the priests, and Jesus is our High Priest, our Mediator. He stands between us and the enemy.

Jesus has done the work for us. It was completed on the cross, where He then cried, *"It is finished"* (John 19:30). He set us free through His sacrifice on Calvary.

The Power of the Name of Jesus

It is because of this that we can effectively use the name of Jesus. We are sealed with that name, and that name rules our lives—internally and externally. Therefore, demons must obey when we use that name.

> *Jesus is our High Priest, our Mediator. He stands between us and the enemy!*

Some people use the name of Jesus when they're not worthy to use it. If you haven't been sealed with that name, then don't use it. You don't have that authority.

You can't fool demons; they know if you have authority or not. You can sometimes fool the people around you, but never the devil or his minions.

The Significance of the Rams' Horns

The seven rams' horns are a picture of redemption. When Abraham took his only son Isaac and went up to Mt. Moriah to offer the child up to God, he was willing in his heart to make this most costly of sacrifices. God, seeing Abraham's willingness, called his attention to a ram caught in the bushes, and Abraham was able to offer that animal instead.

The ram, or male sheep, was known to be the strongest of all sheep, the best of the best, and therefore it became a widely used sacrifice—even in the Temple to be built later in Jerusalem. Nothing was considered to be a better offering to God than a ram. Therefore, when God saw the willingness of Abraham's heart, He gave him the perfect sacrifice, and He does the same for each of us.

The strength of the ram was symbolized by its great horns, and it was these horns, this symbol of strength and perfection, that God ordained to be used when His people went out to battle. The strength of the Perfect Sacrifice was to go before them, and the priests were to make a continual sound on the rams' horns to remind the people of their significance. It was the voice of triumph being heard, and its message was: God is our Deliverer.

The Significance of the Ark

The positioning of the Ark of the Covenant was also important. It was there, in the Ark, that God chose to dwell. The fullness of His presence was there. In the Ark, the Israelites kept several items that reminded them of God's greatness. A pot filled with manna collected in the wilderness reminded them of God's continual provision. Aaron's rod that budded reminded them of God's power and life. The tables on which the Lord had written the Ten Commandments with His own finger on Mt. Sinai reminded them of His Law, of which Christ was the fulfillment. As this Ark passed before them, its presence strengthened them.

The Seventh Day Was Different

Thus ended the second day of marching:

On the second day they compassed the city enclosure once and returned to the camp.

Joshua 6:14

The third day, the fourth, the fifth and the sixth all ended in the very same way:

So they did for six days.   Joshua 6:14

The seventh day, or day of perfection, was to be the all-important day. It would be the day of seeing the fruits of their labors, a day different from all other days:

> *On the seventh day they rose early at daybreak and marched around the city as usual, only on that day they compassed the city seven times. And the seventh time, when the priests had blown the trumpets, Joshua said to the people, Shout! For the Lord has given you the city. And the city and all that is in it shall be devoted to the Lord [for destruction]; only Rahab the harlot and all who are with her in her house shall live, because she hid the messengers whom we sent.*
>
> Joshua 6:15-17

> *They took the city without a shot being fired!*

(Notice that Rahab was still being called *"the harlot"* because she hadn't been redeemed yet. Later, she would lose that title forever and be remembered in a totally different way.) Would this be just a "usual" day? Not in any sense of the word.

Avoiding Contamination

Joshua told the people they were about to take the city, but he warned them not to be contaminated by the things they would find there:

But you keep yourselves from the accursed and devoted things, lest when you have devoted it [to destruction], you take of the accursed thing, and so make the camp of Israel accursed and trouble it. But all the silver and gold and vessels of bronze and iron are consecrated to the Lord; they shall come into the treasury of the Lord.   Joshua 6:18-19

When God gives you victory over your enemies, the danger always exists that you will be lured by the things you see around you, things that are not good for a child of God, and you will want them. This is the quickest way to break covenant with the Lord, the quickest way to lose your Jerichos, the quickest way to lose your victory. Never touch *"the accursed thing."*

That's sound advice in any generation. Touching *"accursed"* things, Joshua warned, would bring trouble, and not only to the individual who was guilty of it. It would trouble the whole camp. Be advised, saints. This is still true today.

"The People Shouted"

The people agreed and did as they were told: *So the people shouted, and the trumpets were blown. When the people heard the sound of the trumpet, they raised a great shout, and [Jericho's] wall fell down in its place, so that the [Israelites] went up into the city, every man straight before him, and they took the city.*

Joshua 6:20

The horns were blown, and when the people heard it, *"they raised a great shout."* That was the shout of a new thing, a shout born of obedience to a new call issued to a new generation of people. And that shout resulted in a miracle that made possible the possession they had so long waited for.

"They Took the City"

"They took the city." They didn't fight among themselves over who would have what and who would do what when. Together, they raised a great shout, together marched forward and together they took the city.

It didn't take the Israelites four days of struggle to take the city. They did spend seven days marching around it, but when the moment for victory came, the city was theirs—without a fight. Today we would say, "They took it without a shot being fired."

Among the Israelites, no one was playing around that day. No one was sulking over having been offended by another. They stood together, and together they took the city.

No one argued about who should do what and how. God had said that they should each march straight forward, and that's what they did. The result was: *"they took the city."*

When they did what they had been instructed to do, they were amazed to find that the Lord of the Hosts had been there before them, and the battle was over. Each man was in his proper place, each man did as he was told, and so *"they took the city."*

Nothing Seemed to Be Happening

That first day, as they marched around the walls of the city, nothing seemed to happen. The same can be said of the second day, the third day, the fourth day, the fifth day and the sixth day. Even after they had marched around seven times on the seventh day, the walls still had not visibly changed. They were in their place, and they were just as strong as ever.

But late on the seventh day, when the trumpets were blown and that great shout went up, suddenly something did happen. Those once impregnable walls suddenly fell down, and they fell down flat, or in their place, so that it was very easy to cross over them.

The Mighty Men of Jericho Were Terrified

The mighty men of Jericho must have been struck with terror and confusion because the Bible describes the aftermath of this event in these words:

And they utterly destroyed all that was in the city, both man and woman, young and old, ox, sheep, and donkey, with the edge of the sword.

Joshua 6:21

When the walls fell, the Israelites were right there. The citizens of Jericho must have wondered what on earth these strange people were doing. They didn't seem to have a clear battle plan, and they had no visible weapons.

Did you read about any weapons being used at Jericho? No? Me neither. I read about the Ark, the priests and the trumpets, but nothing about weapons. These people were armed with nothing but the presence of God.

But that was enough. It is the presence of God that will get you through. It's His presence that will conquer every enemy, destroy every foe and bring down every stronghold.

The Israelites didn't need weapons. All they had to do was shout, and the walls began to tremble and then collapsed.

The Walls "Fell Down Flat"

Most walls, if they fall, fall to one side or they fall in a heap, and going over that fallen wall is difficult. This wall didn't fall in either of those ways. It fell down *"flat,"* and it was easily crossed over.

How could that possibly happen? The only explanation is that the walls sunk into the earth below them, and that's unheard of. Some walls experience a weakening of their foundations over time, and elements of them settle and sink a little. But for the entire wall on every side of the city to sink so rapidly was historic. And for the wall to sink so much that you could walk over the top of it was totally out of sync with the nature of things. This was a

> *That was the shout of a new thing, a shout born of obedience to a new call issued to a new generation of people!*

GREAT miracle, and it terrified the already nervous citizens of Jericho.

God Will Make Your Way Easy

God does not make it hard for you to possess what He has prepared for you. Just the opposite is true. He removes every barrier so that you can just walk in and take what is yours. If you're in the right place, you're willing to be obedient and God's presence is in your life, it will not be impossible or difficult for you to enter in and claim what is yours. If God said it was yours, then it's yours. If God said you could have it, then you can have it. If God said He wanted you to take it, what are you waiting for?

These people didn't have to climb over rubble to get into the city. Their way was made easy. They went in and *"they took the city,"* and it's time that you and I rose up and did the same.

Far too many of us have settled for second best. Far too many of us struggle to possess what is ours. It's time to surrender it all to the Lord of Hosts. The battle belongs to Him.

Most of us have had such terrible experiences with battle that we cringe with the very thought of fighting another one. But when we know that the battle is the Lord's and that the Lord of Hosts is with us, we can relax, stop dreading the battle and just face every enemy squarely, knowing that we shall be victorious.

Many Christians are terrified by the devil. When they mention his name, it's with fear and awe. He's after them all day long, and they're continually running from him. If you will just turn and face the enemy, you'll be surprised to see him turn and run away from you.

Yes! Don't be afraid of any enemy. None can stand against our God. Face every battle with pleasure, knowing that God has won it for you in advance.

Our thinking has to change. The Kingdom of God is not about you, so get over your sulking. There's a higher purpose involved in this battle Every battle we face is about the God inside of us and about what He has invested in us. It's about His anointing and what He wants to do through you. It's not about you; it's about God's call upon you.

"Woe is me! Just look what the devil's done!" We hear people saying much too often. And yet the Israelites just walked in and took control of the city.

It's time to cross over. This is your day. Cross over your Jordans. Cross over the walls of your Jerichos and take dominion of your cities. Cross over into enemy territory. Cross over into possession.

Leave the past behind. You may have to give up some things, but so what? Don't wait for God to demand them of you. Give them up willingly and joyfully so that you can move on to the new and better things God has in store.

Jericho, Shut Up

> It's time for you to shout, "Jericho, shut up!"

And now, it's time for you to shout, "Jericho, shut up!" And that's the end of it. Once you have crossed over, don't go back for any reason. There's nothing back there for you. If you go back and look things over again, worrying about it, making it your battle, fighting it over and over again, you'll find yourself in deep trouble. Always go forward, never backward.

There Was So Much More

This was just a beginning for the children of Israel. There were many lands lying before them yet to be conquered. And the same is true with us. Go on to greater things. Don't settle somewhere before you get all that is yours.

There is much more, and we have settled for something less. We have accepted our current situations as being God's best, and that's usually not the case. There is more out ahead of us—if we'll only be willing to go after it.

What you have now is not God's best, and it never will be. There's more. There's a higher purpose, something deeper, richer and fuller. Go for it. What do you have to lose?

Stop Going Back and Forth

Some Christians are up and down and back and forth with their life. They get a little ahead, and then they plunge way behind again.

Some do this with their family. Just when they think they're making some headway, things seem to fall apart. "Lord, what's happening?" they wonder.

Some people do this with their physical body. They receive a wonderful healing, but then they slip right back into sickness again.

Some do it with ministry. They seem to take a few steps forward, and then they suddenly plunge backward. And they're not sure why this has happened.

Some struggle in this way with their businesses. They need to declare, "Jericho, shut up. You will not prevent me from entering my Canaan. I will walk over you." Then do it. Stop going back and forth and press on into possession.

It's All in Stepping Over

I could tell you today to shout, but it was not the shout that was important that seventh day. The shout, in fact, was not necessary at all.

I could tell you to blow a trumpet, but that's not necessary either.

The morning I was preaching this message to our people, I asked the Lord what we should do to activate the truth of it in our lives. "Should we march around seven times?" I asked.

"It's not necessary," He said.

"Should we give a great shout?" I asked.

"It's not necessary," He said.

"Should we blow a trumpet?" I asked.

"It's not necessary," He answered again.

By that time I was confused. "Well, then, what shall we do, Lord?" I asked.

His answer was clear and concise: "It's simply a matter of stepping over."

That was it. We could have shouted and marched and blown trumpets and never stepped over. The stepping over was the critical part. That's what we all needed to do. If we did everything else and didn't step over, it wouldn't be enough.

That's the important thing. Step over. Do it today. Do it without delay.

If you need some cutting off of the old, then by all means, do that now. If you need some time in your tent to heal, then by all means, do that. If you need to partake of some new manna, then by all means do it. But whatever you do, don't fail to step over. It's stepping-over time.

It's a new day for a new generation, so step over today and take control of your territory. You may not feel anything at all, and you may not see the importance of doing this, but if you'll give it a try, the Lord will be there to meet you.

Tell your Jericho today to "Shut Up!" and then take the prophetic act of stepping over. When you do that, you're speaking to your Jericho. It cannot prevent you from taking your Promised Land. So take a step into the new, and you will come into attainment.

Jericho is yours. God has given it to you.

CHAPTER 8

Occupying Your Canaans

Give me this mountain.   Joshua 14:12, NKJ

Caleb's Story

There's a wonderful story behind Caleb's plea to Joshua, and it goes back to that first time Moses had sent out the spies. God gave him specific instructions for doing so:

And the Lord said to Moses, Send men to explore and scout out [for yourselves] the land of Canaan, which I give to the Israelites. From each tribe of their fathers you shall send a man, every one a leader or head among them. Numbers 13:1

Moses obeyed:

So Moses by the command of the Lord sent scouts from the Wilderness of Paran, all of them men who were heads of the Israelites. Numbers 13:2

Moses sent them to scout out the land of Canaan, and said to them, Get up this way by the South (the Negeb) and go up into the hill country, and see what the land is and whether the people who dwell there are strong or weak, few or many, and whether the land they live in is good or bad, and whether the cities they dwell in are camps or strongholds, and what the land is, whether it is fat or lean, whether

*there is timber on it or not. And be of good courage
and bring some of the fruit of the land.*

Numbers 13:17-20

The children of Israel had been traversing the
wilderness for some time, and they were hoping
for something new. They had a hankering to see
some trees.

How about you? Would you
like to see something you haven't
seen for a while? Or are you satis-
fied with life as it is?

*Would
you
like
to
see
something
you
haven't
seen
for
a
while?*

Needed: Courage

Moses gathered his group of
trusted men and said to them,
"Be of good courage." It meant
for them to establish their courage before they set out on this
mission. They would need their
courage in place.

The root of the phrase *have courage* means "to have
heart," and the word *discouraged,* from the same root,
means "to have your heart ripped out of you." These
men would need heart to complete their assignment,
and you will too.

The Importance of Fruit

"Bring [home] some of the fruit of the land," Moses added. He didn't ask the men to bring back any captives, any enemy weapons or any enemy spoil. He was interested in the land. "Examine the fruit, and bring some of it home for us to examine too."

Fruit is always the important thing, and God has called each of us to be both fruit bearers and fruit examiners.

A "Wow" Time, Forty Critical Days

At this point, the Bible threw in a little interesting tidbit:

Now the time was the time of the first ripe grapes.
Numbers 13:20

The time of the first ripe grapes kicked off a period of rejoicing, or celebration. Wine would be made, and parties would be organized. It was a "WOW" season, just the right time for God's people to see the land!

So they went up and scouted through the land from the Wilderness of Zin to Hebob, to the entrance of Hamath.
Numbers 13:21

I'm sure those men could have written a book about their experiences. They stayed for forty critical days.

And they returned from scouting out the land after forty days. Numbers 13:25

Those forty days were extremely critical and could have spared the people from forty years of wandering—if the men involved had come back with the right kind of report.

Something Positive

They did have something positive to say. The fruit of the land was unquestionably wonderful:

They came to Moses and Aaron and to all the Israelite congregation in the Wilderness of Paran at Kadesh, and brought them word, and showed them the land's fruit. Numbers 13:26

These two things, word and fruit, cannot be separated. I hear people who should know better saying, "I'm tired of trying to please men. From now on, I'm going to live like I want to—whether people like it or not." People who say that are just looking for an excuse to sin. God doesn't want you to be a people-pleaser, but He encourages others around you to examine the fruit of your life. So if you're just cruising through life, living any old way you choose, be assured that God will hold you accountable for every person you offend along the way and everyone you cause to stumble by your disobedience.

The land was just like God said it would be, flowing with milk and honey!

The "But" of Their Report

The land and its fruit were good, just as God had said:

They told Moses, We came to the land to which you sent us; surely it flows with milk and honey. This is its fruit. Numbers 13:27

So far, this seemed to be a WOW report! The land was just like God said it would be, flowing with milk and honey. To prove it, they had the fruit. "BUT" they had something to add, and this was not a good 'but':

But the people who dwell there are strong, and the cities are fortified and very large; moreover, there we saw the sons of Anak [of great stature and courage]. Numbers 13:28

As we noted in an earlier chapter, the spies were divided. Two of them, Joshua and Caleb, emphasized the fruit they had seen. "Yes, there were some giants in the land, but you should have seen the fruit. It was unbelievable." The majority, however, the other ten spies, emphasized the giants. "Yes, there was some good fruit in the land, but you should have seen the giants. They were unbelievable." Alas, the majority report prevailed, and it upset the people terribly, causing them to weep all night. The next day they decided to go back to Egypt, and when Joshua and Caleb tried to dissuade them, they spoke of stoning the two men of faith. When you make a decision to cross over and follow hard after your promises, there are always those who are not on your side. It's sad when they should know better, but that's just the way it often is.

Joshua and Caleb had done nothing wrong. They had risked their lives to bring back a good report, and that good report had been rejected. Now they wanted to encourage the people, and rather than accept their word, the people wanted to stone them.

Not everyone will be happy about the stand you take in life. Not everyone will be happy about how you raise your children. Not everyone will be happy about where you go to church and what your doctrinal position is. When God raises you up and gives you a ministry, not everyone will be happy about that. Some won't like your ministry and will consider that you don't deserve where you're going.

Stop expecting everyone to agree with what you think and what you do. It won't happen. There will always be someone against you for no other reason than that you're full of God. Get used to it.

Caleb Found a Place in God's Heart

This all led to an entire generation being left behind. Still, among those of the older generation, Caleb had found a place in God's heart:

> *Surely they will not see the land which I swore to their fathers; nor shall any who provoked (spurned, despised) Me see it. But my servant Caleb, because he has a different spirit and has followed Me fully, I will bring into the land into which he went, and his descendants shall possess it.* Numbers 14:23-24

As the years passed and one-by-one, the other Israelites of the older generation died off in the wilderness, most of them having forgotten completely the promise of the land, Caleb remained firm. He wanted what was his—no matter how long it took to get it. Then, when it came time to divide up the land, he quickly presented his case before Joshua:

Then the people of Judah came to Joshua in Gilgal, and Caleb son of Jephunneh the Kennezite said to him, You know what the Lord said to Moses the man of God concerning me and you in Kadesh-barnea. Forty years old was I when Moses the servant of the Lord sent me from Kadesh-barnea to scout out the land. And I brought him a report as it was in my heart. But my brethren who went up with me made the hearts of the people melt; yet I wholly followed the Lord my God. And Moses swore on that day, Surely the land on which your feet have walked shall be an inheritance to you and your children always, because you have wholly followed the Lord my God.

And now, behold, the Lord has kept me alive, as He said, these forty-five years since the Lord spoke this word to Moses, while the Israelites wandered in the wilderness; and now, behold, I am this day eighty-five years old. Yet I am as strong today as I was the day Moses sent me; as my strength was then, so is my strength now for war and to go out and to come in. So now give me this hill country of which the Lord spoke that day. For you heard then how the [giantlike] Anakim were there and that the cities were great and fortified; if the Lord will

be with me, I shall drive them out just as the
Lord said. Joshua 14:6-12

The new generation had crossed into Canaan, and now they had to decide what they each wanted. They had certain lands assigned to them, but could they possibly shoot even higher? Could they maybe be allowed to go beyond the expected? Could they have more then others had settled for? Could they perhaps tap into some surprises that God had reserved just for them? Caleb dared to dream big.

Dare to Dream Big

The dream God has given us is bigger than we are, and yet He has surprises in store that we know nothing of yet. We can't imagine how God could ever pay for such things, but He knows how to do it. If God has given you a dream, He can pay for that dream, and if He has reserved surprises for you, you need not worry that His supply will somehow run dry.

But some of us are too timid to reach for our dreams because there are those who we know will object. They would be sure that our dreams are way too big. There is often something hidden deep within us that we are fearful to express because others might think we have "gone off the deep end." We can see their eyeballs rolling already, and we can imagine what they might be thinking. Yet, that hidden dream may be the higher part of God's will for our lives.

One Man Dared to Dream Bigger Dreams

One of our church members was praying at the altar one Sunday morning, and when I asked him what he needed from God, he told me he was asking God for a job. As I ministered to him, the Lord told me to tell him that he was asking too small. He was asking to be hired by someone else to work, but God wanted him to have people working for him. "Tell him 'franchises,' " the Lord said, and I did that.

> *Some of us are too timid to reach for our dreams!*

Not long afterward, this brother was approached by someone with a wonderful idea for franchising. The brother didn't have the money to do it, but the other man said he would put up the necessary investment. All of us who knew our brother and knew his situation also knew that this was a great miracle. A few months later, the brother was hosting our men's fellowship in his brand new home. Our God is great!

God will allow your inheritance to be just as big as you will dare to dream. The problem is that most of us are willing to settle for a lot less, and so we do.

Caleb Had a Good Memory

Caleb had a good memory. He never forgot what Moses had said to him forty-five years earlier, and he was not about to settle for anything less than he had been promised at the time. Now he reminded Joshua. Maybe Joshua had forgotten, but Caleb had not.

At the time the promise was made, things didn't look good for its fulfillment. The majority of the spies had given such a bad report that it had moved the entire nation and caused them to miss out on their inheritance. Still, Caleb knew that they could have all that God had promised.

Wandering can dim your memory and kill your dreams, but Caleb didn't let it happen. Forty-five years of trials and tests in the wilderness have a way of hardening even the best of believers, but Caleb didn't let it happen. He remembered, and now he reminded others.

One Personal Assessment Differs from Another

The spies were sent out as scouts. They were to scout out the land, and they were to bring back their personal assessment of it. Since different men look at any given situation differently, their assessments were not all the same. Joshua and Caleb based their assessment on what God had said to them, while the other ten spies based their assessments on what they had seen in the land. Everyone was welcome to his own opinion. It just so happened that the majority of them had a bad opinion. And that affected everyone.

To the men of faith, the giants were not a problem. They called them *"bread for us"* and declared that their defenses and the *"shadow [or mere appearance] of protection"* that seemed to rest over them was *"removed."*

How could these men give such a report? Joshua had the key. He said that his report came from the *"heart,"* and the report of the majority clearly came from their minds. Even when the majority agreed that there was no way they could conquer the land, Joshua and Caleb remained firm. They *"wholly followed the Lord their God"* and were not swayed by the thinking of the multitude.

Of those who rebelled that day, God said, *"Surely they will not see the land." Surely* was His guarantee. Whatever it took, these men would not cross over and possess the land—on His word.

A Sure Word Over Caleb

God also spoke a sure word through Moses to Caleb that day:

Surely the land on which your feet have walked shall be an inheritance to you and your children always, because you have wholly followed the Lord my God.

> "Wholly" following God leaves no room for any other lover!

This phrase, *"wholly followed the Lord,"* is an important one. That's why it's repeated several times. Your inheritance will depend on whom you are wholly following. This means that there can be nothing between you and God.

Wholly following the Lord is more serious than a mere commitment and more serious than a mere conviction. God wants more than commitment, and He wants more than conviction. He wants you so close that you *"wholly"* follow Him. That means that a spouse doesn't come before God, and a child doesn't come before Him either.

A job can never come before God, a career can never come before God and a ministry can never come before God. Your future cannot come before God. *"Wholly"* leaves no room for anything that competes for His attention.

God has to be first in everything that we do, and His opinion always takes precedence. To *"wholly"* follow God is not something the average Christian is ready to do, but that's what it takes to claim your inheritance.

"Wholly" following God leaves no room for any other lover. He is and must always be the Lover of our Souls. That's why idolatry is the same as adultery with other gods. You can't run around on God, deciding each week which lover you like best. It's either Him alone, or you can forget that special inheritance.

Kept Alive for a Purpose

"The Lord has kept me alive," Caleb said, and many of us can say the same. Without the Lord, we would have been dead a long time ago. And the fact that God has kept us alive should tell us something. He has kept us alive for a purpose.

God has kept us alive for our inheritance. He has kept us alive for His hidden blessings. He has kept us alive for His surprises.

I could have died in so many ways, but I didn't. I'm still alive. I could have been overwhelmed, overloaded and overcome, but the Lord kept me alive. So many things could have ruled me out of the game, but I'm still standing. He kept me alive. So many things could have dragged me down, but it didn't happen. He kept me alive.

And why did God keep me alive? He wanted to give me His inheritance. He didn't want to lose that joy, that pleasure, that blessing me brings to His heart.

God kept me alive for this moment. This is my reason for living. I'm moving into my full inheritance because I have *"wholly followed"* the Lord, and He has kept me alive for this moment.

Can you imagine clinging to a promise like that for forty-five years? That's phenomenal! Most people give up all dreams long before they reach Caleb's age. He was eighty-five years old, and he had not given up on any of his dreams. In fact, he said that he was just as strong at eighty-five as he had been the day Moses had chosen him to spy out the land. That's pretty wonderful!

Caleb had maintained his faith in God and his faith in God's promises, and now he declared: "Give me this mountain. It's mine, and I want it."

Caleb was aware of the fact that no territory would be possessed easily. He knew about the giants there and about the fortified cities. He had seen them for himself. Still, he wasn't afraid of gi-ants—even at eighty-five. *"I shall drive them out just as the Lord said,"* he declared, and everyone knew he meant what he said.

Remember now that Caleb was from a previous generation, and most of his fellow Israelites had died on the other side of Jordan. Why had God kept Caleb alive? He had the nature of the new generation. His thinking had never become corrupted by the nay-sayers on the other side. So they had died, but he had lived.

And he got his mountain:

Then Joshua blessed him and gave Hebron to Caleb son of Jephunneh for an inheritance. So Hebron became the inheritance of Caleb son of Jephunneh the Kennizzite to this day, because he wholly followed the Lord, the God of Israel. The name of Hebron before was Kiriath-arba [city of Arba]. This Arba was the greatest of the Anakim. And the land had rest from war.

Joshua 14:13-15

Here that phrase is again: *"he wholly followed the Lord."* This statement is made fully six times in the Old Testament about Caleb.

Hebron had originally been named for a giant, the greatest of them — Arba. Now, suddenly, *"the land had rest from war."* That was because of the coming of a man who *"wholly followed the Lord."*

Caleb's Commitment Brought Joy to His Life

Caleb had a commitment to *"wholly follow the Lord,"* and we must make the same commitment. Because of his commitment, he had a confidence. He saw the giants, but his confidence in God would not allow him to fear them or change his plans because of them. And he never strayed from his confidence. He knew what God had said, and He knew that God would do what He said He would do.

Many Bible characters had songs they sang, and I believe Caleb had one too:

> *I want that mountain,*
> *I want that mountain,*
> *Where the milk and honey flows*
> *Where grapes are huge and are carried in on*
> *poles.*
> *Give me my mountain!*

Somehow I can picture Caleb as he came back from those forty days of spying out the land. I see him dancing along as he rejoiced in the wonderful fruit of the land that was to be his. Those grapes were so large that it took only a few to make a wonderful glass of wine. How he rejoiced!

Something Terrible Intervened

Then something terrible intervened, and that dream was delayed for many years, too many years, more years than most of us would dare to keep believing. But when the Israelites had crossed Jordan, conquered the border cities and begun to divide up the land, Caleb was still dancing. He had never lost sight of his mountain, and he was about to possess it at last.

> *Will you accept a small lot, or will you contend for a whole mountain?*

Caleb was committed, he was confident and he had courage. Many of us whine and complain over the smallest of things, but Caleb was ready to face giants. Most of what we focus on is nothing. God will take care of it.

The giants didn't "wow" Caleb. He was more "wowed" about the fruit than he was with the giants. And, when many years had passed, he knew that his having gray hair didn't change God or His promises. That meant nothing. Age can defeat us only if we allow it to do so.

What Was Going On?

It didn't even matter how long Caleb had to sit and wait for the promise. What was he doing all those years? He must have busied himself with the mundane affairs of daily life, but in the back of his mind, he always knew that none of it mattered. He had a clear picture of his mountain, and he was going to have it—whatever the cost.

As the days turned into weeks, the weeks into months, and the months into years, and time began to stamp itself upon his features, it would have been understandable if Caleb had given up on his dreams. But not him. Nothing changed God, and his dreams depended on God, so they couldn't die either.

When his sons had their sons, and he began to be called Pawpaw, it would have been understandable if he had lost sight of his dreams. But not him. God was the Ancient of Days, and He never changed. Caleb held on tight to his dreams and waited for a better day. Now he, his children and his grandchildren would all enjoy their slice of the Promised Land together.

He still had the ability to take a mountain, and God had promised him a mountain, so why settle for less? "Give me my mountain!"

He had the commitment, the confidence, and the courage, and he had the conquest. "Give me this mountain." Some of you have crossed over, but you've settled for far less than is yours. Will you accept a small lot, or will you contend for a whole mountain?

Don't settle for something small. Don't settle for a cup of milk when God wants to give you the whole dairy herd. Don't settle for a taste of honey, when God wants to give you the whole hive.

There Was One Very Big Difference

Because everyone else was prevented from going into the Promised Land for many years, Caleb was too. As they went round and round in the wilderness, he had to go round and round with them. But there was one big difference. They died and never saw their dreams fulfilled. Caleb lived and went on to take his mountain. He knew what God had told him, and he would not give it up for any man.

Until that day came, Caleb had to put up with a lot of griping people, but he didn't let it get him down. He maintained his integrity before God in the midst of it all.

What Are You Claiming?

Now that you've crossed over, what will you claim as your own? If you cross over, but you don't know what you want, what good is the crossing over? If you don't have a dream bigger than yourself, then it's not worth crossing over. If all you want is to get enough manna to exist day by day, you can get that on the other side of Jordan.

> *When will you begin to eat of the good of the land?*

You're in the land flowing with milk and honey. When will you begin to eat of the good of the land? When will you begin to take what is yours? When will you lay hold of your full inheritance?

Get your sights raised. Get your thinking straightened out. You're a child of the King, so start acting like it.

Think big. Act big. Walk tall.

Get beyond just asking God to help you pay your electric bill. Go beyond mere necessities. Those are guaranteed in the package. Get into the extras, the special blessings, the secrets God has stored up for you. It's time to go beyond.

Caleb Got His Mountain

As long as Caleb had to wait, he still knew that mountain was his. How did that happen? He had to keep reminding himself of what God had said. He had to keep believing that what God said was true. He had to keep visualizing his land as he had seen it, and he had to keep moving forward toward it, even as he put up with all the nonsense around him. Remember his neighbors had, at one point, wanted to stone him.

The end of the story is that Caleb got his mountain, and that's the important part. You cannot afford to settle for a mere lot, when God has promised you a mountain. So what have you asked God for?

You've probably asked very little, for only a portion of God's will for you. But He's God, so why not ask big? Why not ask for much more? If He's given you the dream, then believe Him for the fulfillment. If He has given you the dream, what makes you think that He cannot accomplish it?

Until now, you've asked way too small because your thinking is too small. God said:

For as [a man] thinks in his heart, so is he.
Proverbs 23:7

If you think small, then you'll ask small, and if you think big, then you'll ask big. It up to you. What do you want for your inheritance? Please don't be content with anything less than your portion. Let every box be removed from your thinking, and let God enlarge you today. It's your day for possessing.

CHAPTER 9

What Are We Birthing?

After the death of Moses the servant of the Lord, the Lord said to Joshua, son of Nun, Moses' minister, Moses My servant is dead. So now arise [take his place], go over this Jordan, you and all this people, into the land which I am giving to them, the Israelites.

Joshua 1:1-2

It's a New Day

Beloved, it's a new day. How we used to think, what we used to do and how we used to do it are no longer relevant. As we press into God, we sense that we are birthing something in the Spirit realm, but we don't yet know what it is.

In the days before ultrasound, we had to wait until a child was born before we could know what we had brought forth. So it is in the Spirit realm today. We may not have held our child yet and stroked it and kissed it, but we have felt the change. Something has been born, and we will soon see the nature of it.

When a woman gives birth to a child, she suddenly awakens to find herself in unfamiliar surroundings. Everything is bloody from the process, and instruments are strewn here and there. It's not a pretty scene. Still, her heart is filled with joy, for she knows that a new life has come into the world.

The chaos of her surroundings is temporary. She will soon be taking her baby home with her. She has been in that place just long enough to get the job done and get her to the next level. And that next level will soon come.

If she looks at the circumstances around her, she might think that nothing has changed. She knows that she's been through some real battles in a real wilderness, and that she's had some bad experiences. That a change has come is not yet apparent.

But it soon will be. Her pain had a purpose. Her travail led to something. She will soon hold it in her arms. It is even now coming through the door in the arms of another. The birthing room is all about destiny and purpose. And, trust me, it will be worth it all.

From this day forward, begin to cross over and possess as never before. If that is your desire, then I want to offer this prayer for you today:

Father,

I pray that every heart will be open to what You are saying to the Church in this hour. Let everything that disturbs and hinders us be pushed aside, and let us be free to cross over this day into all that You have prepared for us.

Amen!

Ministry Page

You may contact Pastor Regina Blount in any of the following ways.

Regina Blount
P.O. Box 1742
Hammond, LA 70404

rablount@bellsouth.net

www.alchammond.org

THE 7th LEVEL

Taking Your Faith to the Level of Perfection

LLOYD W. BLOUNT

www.ingramcontent.com/pod-product-compliance
Lightning Source LLC
LaVergne TN
LVHW011328080426
835513LV00006B/244